Test-Driven iOS De
with Swift 4

Third Edition

Write Swift code that is maintainable, flexible, and easily extensible

Dr. Dominik Hauser

BIRMINGHAM - MUMBAI

MW00846663

Test-Driven iOS Development with Swift 4

Third Edition

First published: February 2016

Second edition: October 2016

Third edition: October 2017

Production reference: 1271017

Published by Packt Publishing Ltd.
Livery Place
35 Livery Street
Birmingham
B3 2PB, UK.

ISBN 978-1-78847-570-9

www.packtpub.com

Credits

Author
Dr. Dominik Hauser

Reviewer
S Ravi Shankar

Commissioning Editor
Kunal Chaudhari

Acquisition Editor
Reshma Raman

Content Development Editor
Jason Pereira

Technical Editor
Prajakta Mhatre

Copy Editors
Charlotte Carneiro
Safis Editing

Project Coordinator
Sheejal Shah

Proofreader
Safis Editing

Indexer
Francy Puthiry

Production Coordinator
Shraddha Falebhai

About the Author

Dr. Dominik Hauser completed his PhD in physics from the University of Heidelberg. While working as a university professor, he started iOS development in his spare time. His first app on physics has been an astounding success worldwide. Since then, he has turned himself into a full-time iOS developer, with a number of successful apps to his name. He has been a Swift developer since day one and runs a blog on iOS development.

About the Reviewer

S Ravi Shankar is a multi-skilled software consultant with over 17+ years of experience in IT industry. He has a good all-around ability to work in different technologies and extensive experience in product development, system maintenance, and support. He is a polyglot and a self-taught programmer with hands-on experience in Swift, Objective-C, and Java.

It was a pleasure to work with Sheejal, project coordinator at Packt, and thanks to Packt for giving me this opportunity.

www.PacktPub.com

For support files and downloads related to your book, please visit www.PacktPub.com. Did you know that Packt offers eBook versions of every book published, with PDF and ePub files available? You can upgrade to the eBook version at www.PacktPub.com and as a print book customer, you are entitled to a discount on the eBook copy. Get in touch with us at service@packtpub.com for more details.

At www.PacktPub.com, you can also read a collection of free technical articles, sign up for a range of free newsletters and receive exclusive discounts and offers on Packt books and eBooks.

https://www.packtpub.com/mapt

Get the most in-demand software skills with Mapt. Mapt gives you full access to all Packt books and video courses, as well as industry-leading tools to help you plan your personal development and advance your career.

Why subscribe?

- Fully searchable across every book published by Packt
- Copy and paste, print, and bookmark content
- On demand and accessible via a web browser

Customer Feedback

Thanks for purchasing this Packt book. At Packt, quality is at the heart of our editorial process. To help us improve, please leave us an honest review on this book's Amazon page at https://www.amazon.com/dp/1788475704.

If you'd like to join our team of regular reviewers, you can e-mail us at customerreviews@packtpub.com. We award our regular reviewers with free eBooks and videos in exchange for their valuable feedback. Help us be relentless in improving our products!

Table of Contents

Preface

iOS projects have become bigger and more complex. Many projects have already surpassed desktop applications in their complexity. One important strategy to manage this complexity is through the use of unit tests. By writing tests, a developer can point out the intention of the code and provide a safety net against the introduction of bugs.

By writing tests first (test-driven development), the developer focuses on the problem. This way, they are forced to think about the domain and rephrase a feature request using their own understanding by writing the test. In addition to this, applications are written using TDD only containing code that is necessary to solve the problem.

As a result, the code is clearer, and the developer gains more confidence that the code actually works.

In this book, you will develop an entire iOS app using TDD. You will experience different strategies for writing tests for models, view controller, and networking code.

What this book covers

Chapter 1, *Your First Unit Tests*, walks you through your first unit tests using Xcode and discusses the benefits of using TDD.

Chapter 2, *Planning and Structuring Your Test-Driven iOS App*, introduces the app you are going to write through the course of this book and how to set up a project in Xcode.

Chapter 3, *A Test-Driven Data Model*, discusses the TDD of a data model.

Chapter 4, *A Test-Driven View Controller*, shows you how to write tests for a view controller, and describes how to use fake objects to isolate micro features for the test.

Chapter 5, *Testing Network Code*, teaches you to test network code using stubs to fake a server component before it is developed.

Chapter 6, *Putting It All Together*, walks you through the integration of all the different parts developed in previous chapters and shows the use of functional tests.

Chapter 7, *Code Coverage*, shows you how to measure the code coverage of your tests using Xcode.

Chapter 8, *Where to Go from Here*, wraps up and shows you the possible next steps to improve your acquired testing skills.

What you need for this book

The following hardware and software is needed to follow the code examples in the book:

- Mac with Sierra or above (macOS 10.12)
- Xcode 9

Who this book is for

If debugging iOS apps is a nerve-racking task for you and you are looking for a fix, this book is for you.

Conventions

In this book, you will find a number of text styles that distinguish between different kinds of information. Here are some examples of these styles and an explanation of their meaning.

Code words in text, database table names, folder names, filenames, file extensions, pathnames, dummy URLs, user input, and Twitter handles are shown as follows: "To be able to write tests for your code, you need to import the module with the `@testable` keyword."

A block of code is set as follows:

```
func makeHeadline(string: String) -> String {
  return "This Is A Test Headline"
}
```

When we wish to draw your attention to a particular part of a code block, the relevant lines or items are set in bold:

```
override func setUp() {
  super.setUp()
  viewController = ViewController()
}
```

New terms and **important words** are shown in bold. Words that you see on the screen, for example, in menus or dialog boxes, appear in the text like this: "To edit the build scheme, click on scheme on the toolbar in Xcode, and then click on **Edit Scheme...**."

> Tips and important notes appear in a box like this.

> Tips and tricks appear like this.

Reader feedback

Feedback from our readers is always welcome. Let us know what you think about this book-what you liked or disliked. Reader feedback is important for us as it helps us develop titles that you will really get the most out of. To send us general feedback, simply email feedback@packtpub.com, and mention the book's title in the subject of your message. If there is a topic that you have expertise in and you are interested in either writing or contributing to a book, see our author guide at www.packtpub.com/authors.

Customer support

Now that you are the proud owner of a Packt book, we have a number of things to help you to get the most from your purchase.

Downloading the example code

You can download the example code files for this book from your account at http://www.packtpub.com. If you purchased this book elsewhere, you can visit http://www.packtpub.com/support and register to have the files e-mailed directly to you. You can download the code files by following these steps:

1. Log in or register to our website using your e-mail address and password.
2. Hover the mouse pointer on the **SUPPORT** tab at the top.
3. Click on **Code Downloads & Errata**.
4. Enter the name of the book in the **Search** box.

5. Select the book for which you're looking to download the code files
6. Choose from the drop-down menu where you purchased this book from.
7. Click on **Code Download**.

Once the file is downloaded, please make sure that you unzip or extract the folder using the latest version of:

- WinRAR / 7-Zip for Windows
- Zipeg / iZip / UnRarX for Mac
- 7-Zip / PeaZip for Linux

The code bundle for the book is also hosted on GitHub at `https://github.com/PacktPublishing/Test-Driven-iOS-Development-with-Swift-4-Third-Edition`. We also have other code bundles from our rich catalog of books and videos available at `https://github.com/PacktPublishing/`. Check them out!

Downloading the color images of this book

We also provide you with a PDF file that has color images of the screenshots/diagrams used in this book. The color images will help you better understand the changes in the output. You can download this file from `https://www.packtpub.com/sites/default/files/downloads/TestDriveniOSDevelopmentwithSwift4ThirdEdition_ColorImages.pdf`.

Errata

Although we have taken every care to ensure the accuracy of our content, mistakes do happen. If you find a mistake in one of our books-maybe a mistake in the text or the code-we would be grateful if you could report this to us. By doing so, you can save other readers from frustration and help us improve subsequent versions of this book. If you find any errata, please report them by visiting `http://www.packtpub.com/submit-errata`, selecting your book, clicking on the **Errata Submission Form** link, and entering the details of your errata. Once your errata are verified, your submission will be accepted and the errata will be uploaded to our website or added to any list of existing errata under the Errata section of that title.

To view the previously submitted errata, go to `https://www.packtpub.com/books/content/support` and enter the name of the book in the search field. The required information will appear under the **Errata** section.

Piracy

Piracy of copyrighted material on the Internet is an ongoing problem across all media. At Packt, we take the protection of our copyright and licenses very seriously. If you come across any illegal copies of our works in any form on the internet, please provide us with the location address or website name immediately so that we can pursue a remedy.

Please contact us at `copyright@packtpub.com` with a link to the suspected pirated material.

We appreciate your help in protecting our authors and our ability to bring you valuable content.

Questions

If you have a problem with any aspect of this book, you can contact us at `questions@packtpub.com`, and we will do our best to address the problem.

1
Your First Unit Tests

When the iPhone platform was first introduced, applications were small and focused only on one feature. It was easy to make money with an app that only did just one thing (for example, a flashlight app that only showed a white screen). The code for these apps only had a few hundred lines and could easily be tested by tapping the screen for a few minutes.

Since then, the App Store has changed a lot. Even now, there are small apps with a clear focus in the App Store, but it's much harder to make money from them. A common app is complicated and feature-rich, but still needs to be easy to use. There are companies with several developers per platform working on one app all the time. These apps sometimes have a feature set that is normally found in desktop applications. It is very difficult and time consuming to test all the features on such apps by hand.

One reason for this is that manual testing needs to be done through a user interface, and it takes time to load the app to be tested. In addition to this, human beings are very slow compared to the capabilities of computers. Most of the time, a computer waits for the user's next input. If we could let a computer insert values, testing could be drastically accelerated. Additionally, the computer could test the features of the app without loading the user interface; thus, the complete app could be tested within seconds. This is exactly what unit tests are all about.

Writing unit tests is hard at first because it is a new concept. This chapter is aimed at helping you to get started with unit tests and how they are used in Xcode. We will also discuss **Test-Driven Development (TDD)**, in which the tests are written before the implementation code. We will see how TDD is done in Xcode, and we will discuss its advantages and disadvantages.

We will cover the following topics in this chapter:

- Building your first automatic unit test
- Understanding TDD
- TDD in Xcode
- The advantages of TDD
- The disadvantages of TDD

Building your first automatic unit test

If you have done some iOS development (or application development in general) already, the following example might seem familiar to you.

You are planning to build an app. You start collecting features, drawing some sketches, or your project manager hands the requirements to you. At some point, you start coding. After you have set up the project, you start implementing the required features of the app.

Let's say an app is an input form, and the values the user puts in have to be validated before the data can be sent to the server. The validation checks, for example, whether the email address looks like it's supposed to and the phone number has a valid format. You implement the form and check whether everything works. But before you can test, you need to write code that presents the form on the screen. Then, you build and run your app in the iOS simulator. The form is somewhere deep in the view hierarchy. So, you navigate to this view and put the values into the form. It doesn't work. Next, you go back to the code and try to fix the problem. Sometimes, this also means that you need to run the debugger, and build and run to check whether the code still has errors.

Eventually, the validation works for the test data you put in. Normally, you would need to test for all possible values to make sure that the validation not only works for your name and your data, but also for all valid data. But there is this long list of requirements on your desk, and you are already running late. The navigation to the form takes three taps in the simulator, and putting in all the different values just takes too long. You are a coder after all.

If only a robot could perform this testing for you.

What are unit tests?

Automatic unit tests act like this robot for you. They execute code, but without the need of navigating to the screen with the feature to test. Instead of running the app over and over again, you write tests with different input data and let the computer test your code in the blink of an eye. Let's see how this works in a simple example.

Implementing a unit test example

Open **Xcode** and go to **File | New | Project**. Navigate to **iOS | Application | Single View App**, and click on **Next**. Put in the name `FirstDemo`, select the language **Swift**, and check **Include Unit Tests**. Uncheck **Use Core Data** and **Include UI Tests**, and click on **Next**. The following screenshot shows the options in Xcode:

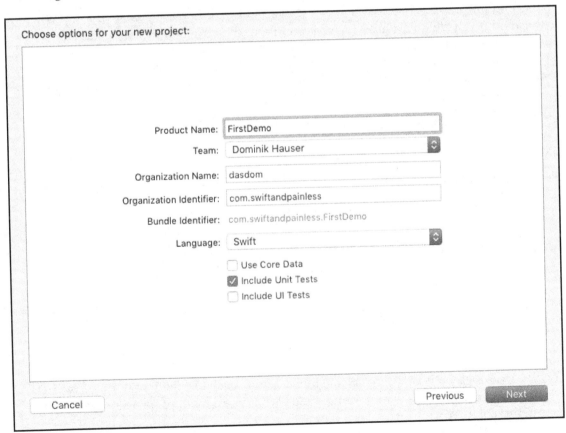

Xcode sets up a project ready for development in addition to a test target for your unit tests. Open the `FirstDemoTests` folder in the Project Navigator. Within the folder, there are two files: `FirstDemoTests.swift` and `Info.plist`. Select `FirstDemoTests.swift` to open it in the editor.

What you see here is a **test case**. A test case is a class comprising several tests. In the beginning, it's good practice to have a test case for each class in the main target.

Let's go through this file step by step:

```
import XCTest
@testable import FirstDemo
```

Every test case needs to import the `XCTest` framework. It defines the `XCTestCase` class and the test assertions that you will see later in this chapter.

The second line imports the module `FirstDemo`. All the code you write for the app will be in this module. By default, classes, structs, enums, and their methods are defined as internal. This means that they can be accessed within the module. But the test code lives outside of the module. To be able to write tests for your code, you need to import the module with the `@testable` keyword. This keyword makes the internal elements of the module accessible to the test case.

Next, we'll take a look at the class declaration:

```
class FirstDemoTests: XCTestCase {
```

Nothing special here. This defines the `FirstDemoTests` class as a subclass of `XCTestCase`.

The first two methods in the class are as follows:

```
override func setUp() {
  super.setUp()
  // Put setup code here. This method is called ...
}

override func tearDown() {
  // Put teardown code here. This method is called ...
  super.tearDown()
}
```

The `setUp()` method is called before the invocation of each test method in the class. Here, you can insert the code that should run before each test. You will see an example of this later in this chapter.

The opposite of `setUp()` is `tearDown()`. This method is called after the invocation of each test method in the class. If you need to clean up after your tests, put the necessary code in this method.

There are two test methods in the template provided by Apple:

```
func testExample() {
    // This is an example of a functional test case.
    // Use XCTAssert and related functions to verify your ...
}

func testPerformanceExample() {
    // This is an example of a performance test case.
    self.measure {
        // Put the code you want to measure the time of here.
    }
}
}
```

The first method is a normal test. You will use this kind of test a lot in the course of this book.

The second method is a performance test. It is used to test methods or functions that perform time-critical computations. The code you put into the `measure` closure is called 10 times, and the average duration is measured. Performance tests can be useful when implementing or improving complex algorithms and to make sure that their performance does not decline. We will not use performance tests in this book.

All the test methods that you write have to have the `test` prefix; otherwise, the test runner can't find and run them. This behavior allows easy disabling of tests--just remove the `test` prefix of the method name. Later, you will take a look at other possibilities to disable some tests without renaming or removing them.

Now, let's implement our first test. Let's assume that you have a method that counts the vowels of a string. A possible implementation looks like this:

```
func numberOfVowels(in string: String) -> Int {
    let vowels: [Character] = ["a", "e", "i", "o", "u",
                               "A", "E", "I", "O", "U"]

    var numberOfVowels = 0
    for character in string {
        if vowels.contains(character) {
            numberOfVowels += 1
        }
    }
}
```

```
    return numberOfVowels
}
```

Add this method to the `ViewController` class in `ViewController.swift`.

This method does the following things:

1. First, an array of characters is defined containing all the vowels in the English alphabet.

 Without the `[Character]` type declaration right after the name of the constant, this would be created as an array of strings, but we need an array of characters here.

2. Next, we define a variable to store the number of vowels. The counting is done by looping over the characters of the string. If the current character is contained in the `vowels` array, `numberOfVowels` is increased by one.
3. Finally, `numberOfVowels` is returned.

Open `FirstDemoTests.swift` methods (the methods with the `test` prefix). Add the following method to it:

```
func test_NumberOfVowels_WhenPassedDominik_ReturnsThree() {
    let viewController = ViewController()

    let string = "Dominik"

    let numberOfVowels = viewController.numberOfVowels(in: string)

    XCTAssertEqual(numberOfVowels, 3,
                   "should find 3 vowels in Dominik")
}
```

 Downloading the example code
You can download the example code files for all Packt books you have purchased from your account at http://www.packtpub.com. If you have purchased this book from elsewhere, you can visit http://www.packtpub.com/support and register to have the files emailed directly to you.

This test creates an instance of `ViewController` and assigns it to the `viewController` constant. It defines a string to use in the test. Then, it calls the function that we want to test and assigns the result to a constant. Finally, the test method calls the `XCTAssertEqual(_, _)` function to check whether the result is what we expected.

To run the tests, go to **Product | Test**, or use the *command + U* shortcut. Xcode compiles the project and runs the test. You will see something similar to what is shown in this screenshot:

```
     func test_NumberOfVowels_WhenPassedDominik_ReturnsThree() {
25     let viewController = ViewController()
26
27     let string = "Dominik"
28
29     let numberOfVowels = viewController.numberOfVowels(in: string)
30
31     XCTAssertEqual(numberOfVowels, 3,
32                     "should find 3 vowels in Dominik")
33   }
```

The green diamond with a checkmark on the left-hand side of the editor indicates that the test passed. So, this is it. This is your first unit test. Step back for a moment and celebrate. This could be the beginning of a new development paradigm for you.

Now that we have a test that proves that the method does what we intended, we are going to improve the implementation. The method looks like it has been translated from Objective-C. But this is Swift. We can do better. Open `ViewController.swift`, and replace the `numberOfVowels(in:)` method with this swifter implementation:

```
func numberOfVowels(in string: String) -> Int {
    let vowels: [Character] = ["a", "e", "i", "o", "u",
                               "A", "E", "I", "O", "U"]

    return string.characters.reduce(0) {
        $0 + (vowels.contains($1) ? 1 : 0)
    }
}
```

Here, we make use of the `reduce` function, which is defined in the array type. Run the tests again (*command + U*), to make sure that this implementation works the same as the one earlier.

Before we move on, let's recap what we have seen so far. First, you learned that you could easily write code that tests your code. Secondly, you saw that a test helped improve the code because now you don't have to worry about breaking the feature when changing the implementation.

To check whether the result of the method is as we expected, we used XCTAssertEqual(_, _). This is one of many XCTAssert functions that are defined in the XCTest framework. The next section shows the most important ones.

Important built-in assert functions

Each test needs to assert some expected behavior. The use of the XCTAssert functions tells Xcode what is expected.

A test method without a XCTAssert function will always pass as long as it compiles.

The most important assert functions are:

- XCTAssertTrue(_:_:file:line:): This asserts that an expression is true
- XCTAssertFalse(_:_:file:line:): This asserts that an expression is false
- XCTAssertEqual(_:_:_:file:line:): This asserts that two expressions are equal
- XCTAssertEqualWithAccuracy(_:_:accuracy:_:file:line:): This asserts that two expressions are the same, taking into account the accuracy defined in the accuracy parameter
- XCTAssertNotEqual(_:_:_:file:line:): This asserts that two expressions are not equal
- XCTAssertNil(_:_:file:line:): This asserts that an expression is a nil
- XCTAssertNotNil(_:_:file:line:): This asserts that an expression is not nil
- XCTFail(_:file:line:): This always fails

To take a look at the full list of the available XCTAssert functions, press *Ctrl*, and click on the XCTAssertEqual word in the test that you have just written. Then, select **Jump to Definition** in the pop-up menu.

Note that all the XCTAssert functions could be written using XCTAssertTrue(_:_:file:line:). For example, these two lines of code are equivalent to each other:

```
// This assertion is equivalent to...
XCTAssertEqual(2, 1+1, "2 should be the same as 1+1")


// ...this assertion
XCTAssertTrue(2 == 1+1, "2 should be the same as 1+1")
```

But you should use the more precise assertions whenever possible. The reason is, the log output of the more precise assertion methods tells you exactly what happened in case of a failure. For example, look at the log output of the following two assertions:

```
XCTAssertEqual(2, 1, "foo")
// Output:
// XCTAssertEqual failed: ("2") is not equal to ("1") - foo


XCTAssertTrue(2 == 1, "bar")
// Output:
// XCTAssertTrue failed - bar
```

In the first case, you don't need to look at the test to understand what happened. The log tells you exactly what went wrong.

In all the XCTAssert functions, the last three parameters are optional. To take a look at an example for the use of all the parameters, let's check out what a failing test looks like in Xcode. Open FirstDemoTests.swift, and change the expected number of vowels from 3 to 4:

```
XCTAssertEqual(numberOfVowels, 4,
                "should find 4 vowels in Dominik")
```

Now, run the tests. The test fails. You will see something like this:

```swift
func test_NumberOfVowels_WhenPassedDominik_ReturnsThree() {
    let viewController = ViewController()

    let string = "Dominik"

    let numberOfVowels = viewController.numberOfVowels(in: string)

    XCTAssertEqual(numberOfVowels, 4,    XCTAssertEqual failed: ("3") is not equal to ("4") -...
                   "should find 4 vowels in Dominik")
}
```

Xcode tells you that something went wrong with this test. Next, to the `test` function in the preceding screenshot, there is a red diamond with an **x** on line number 24. The same symbol is in the line that actually failed. On the right is the explanation of what actually went wrong, followed by the string you provided in the `XCTAssertEqual` function. In this case, the first parameter, `numberOfVowels`, is **3**; and the second parameter is **4**. As 3 is not equal to 4, the test fails.

As mentioned earlier, `XCTAssertEqual(...)` has two more parameters--`file` and `line`. These parameters allow you to alter what is printed in the debug console in case of a test failure. Navigate to **View | Debug Area | Activate Console** and open the debug console. If the debug area is split in half, click on the second right-most button in the bottom-right corner to hide the variables' view:

```
Test Suite 'FirstDemoTests.xctest' started at 2017-08-11 17:10:30.039
Test Suite 'FirstDemoTests' started at 2017-08-11 17:10:30.040
Test Case '-[FirstDemoTests.FirstDemoTests test_NumberOfVowels_WhenPassedDominik_ReturnsThree]' started.
/Users/dom/Documents/TDD_book/edition_03/code/FirstDemo/FirstDemoTests/FirstDemoTests.swift:31: error: -
[FirstDemoTests.FirstDemoTests test_NumberOfVowels_WhenPassedDominik_ReturnsThree] : XCTAssertEqual
failed: ("3") is not equal to ("4") - should find 4 vowels in Dominik
Test Case '-[FirstDemoTests.FirstDemoTests test_NumberOfVowels_WhenPassedDominik_ReturnsThree]' failed
(0.068 seconds).
Test Suite 'FirstDemoTests' failed at 2017-08-11 17:10:30.113.
     Executed 1 test, with 1 failure (0 unexpected) in 0.068 (0.073) seconds
Test Suite 'FirstDemoTests.xctest' failed at 2017-08-11 17:10:30.116.
     Executed 1 test, with 1 failure (0 unexpected) in 0.068 (0.077) seconds
Test Suite 'All tests' failed at 2017-08-11 17:10:30.117.
     Executed 1 test, with 1 failure (0 unexpected) in 0.068 (0.089) seconds

Test session log:
     /var/folders/md/71cqg1rx07d0h3q9yp91hhdr0000gn/T/com.apple.dt.XCTest/IDETestRunSession-FBB  BBD-
B6F4-44DB-A172-A780881D51E7/FirstDemoTests-17EE33C5-EBB5-435F-86F8-C4FA3E28496E/Session-
FirstDemoTests-2017-08-11_170959-PICacn.log
```

All Output ⌄   ⊜ Filter   🗑 | ▢ ▢

We have only one test at the moment, and the debug output is already kind of messy. Later in this chapter, we will learn that there is a better UI for the same information in Xcode.

There is one line in the output that shows the failing test:

```
/Users/dom/Documents/TDD_book/edition_03/code/FirstDemo/FirstDemoTests/Firs
tDemoTests.swift:31: error: -[FirstDemoTests.FirstDemoTests
test_NumberOfVowels_WhenPassedDominik_ReturnsThree] : XCTAssertEqual
failed: ("3") is not equal to ("4") - should find 4 vowels in Dominik
```

The output starts with the file and line where the failing tests are located. With the `file` and `line` parameter of the `XCTAssert` functions, we can alter what is printed there. Go back to the test method, and replace the assertion with this:

```
XCTAssertEqual(numberOfVowels, 4,
               "should find 4 vowels in Dominik",
               file: "FirstDemoTests.swift", line: 24)
```

The test method starts at line number 24.

With this change, the output is as follows:

```
FirstDemoTests.swift:24: error: -[FirstDemoTests.FirstDemoTests
test_NumberOfVowels_WhenPassedDominik_ReturnsThree] : XCTAssertEqual
failed: ("3") is not equal to ("4") - should find 4 vowels in Dominik
```

The debug output of the test now shows the filename and line number that we specified in the assertion function. This doesn't sound like a useful feature, but later in the book, you will see an example where this really shines.

As I mentioned earlier, in all the `XCTAssert` functions, the last three parameters are optional. In cases where you don't need the message because the used assertion function makes clear what the failure is, you can omit it.

Before we move on with the introduction to TDD, change the test so that it passes again.

Understanding TDD

Now that we have seen what unit tests are and how they can help in development, we are going to learn about TDD.

In 1996, Kent Beck introduced a new software development methodology called **Extreme Programming**. The word *Extreme* indicates that the concepts behind Extreme Programming are totally different from the concepts used in software development back then. For many people, these concepts sound extreme even today.

The methodology is based on 12 rules or practices. One of the rules states that developers have to write unit tests and all parts of the software have to be thoroughly tested. All tests have to pass before the software (or a new feature) can be released to customers. The tests should be written before the production code that they test.

This so-called **test-first programming** led to TDD. As the name suggests, in TDD, tests drive the development. This means that the developer writes code only because there is a test that fails. The tests dictate whether the code has to be written, and they also provide a measure when a feature is "done"--it is done when all tests for this feature pass.

Robert C. Martin (known as Uncle Bob) has come up with three simple rules for TDD:

- You are not allowed to write any production code unless it is to pass a failing unit test
- You are not allowed to write any more of a unit test that is sufficient to fail, and compilation failures are failures
- You are not allowed to write any more production code that is sufficient to pass the one failing unit test

 For more information, visit `http://www.butunclebob.com/ArticleS.UncleBob.TheThreeRulesOfTdd`.

These rules sound kind of silly because when you start with a feature that uses a new class or method that is not declared yet, the test will fail immediately, and you have to add some code just to be able to finish writing the test. But by following these rules, you will only write code that is actually needed to implement the features. And you will only write test code that is needed as well. All the code you write will either end up being part of the final product or it will be a part of your test suite.

Because of the focus on just one feature at a time, you will have a working piece of software almost all the time. So, when your boss enters your office and asks you for a demonstration of the current status of the project, you are only a few minutes away from a presentable (that is, compiling), and a thoroughly tested piece of software.

The TDD workflow - red, green, and refactor

The normal workflow of TDD comprises three steps--the red, green, and refactor steps, respectively. The following sections describe these steps in detail.

Red

You start by writing a failing test. It needs to test a required feature of the software product that is not already implemented or an edge case that you want to make sure is covered. The name *red* comes from the way most IDEs indicate a failing test. Xcode uses a red diamond with a white **x** on it.

It is very important that the test you write in this step initially fails. Otherwise, you can't ensure that the test works and really tests the feature that you want to implement. It could be that you have written a test that always passes and is, therefore, useless. Or, it is possible that the feature is already implemented. Either way, you gain insight into your code.

Green

In the *green* step, you write the simplest code that makes the test pass. It doesn't matter whether the code you write is good and clean. The code can also be silly and even wrong. It is enough when all the tests pass. The name *green* refers to how most IDEs indicate a passing test. Xcode uses a green diamond with a white check mark.

It is very important that you try to write the simplest code that makes the tests pass. By doing so, you only write code that you actually need and that is the simplest implementation possible. When I say *simple*, I mean that it should be easy to read, understand, and change. The code should always be easy to understand.

Often the simplest implementation will not be enough for the feature you try to implement, but still enough to make all the tests pass. This just means that you need another failing test to further drive the development of that feature.

Refactor

During the green step, you write just enough code to make all the tests pass again. As I just mentioned, it doesn't matter what the code looks like in the green step. In the refactor step, you should improve the code. You remove duplication, extract common values, and so on. Do what is needed to make the code as good as possible. The tests help you to not break already implemented features while refactoring.

Don't skip this step. Always try to think how you can improve the code after you have implemented a feature. Doing so helps to keep the code clean and maintainable. This ensures that it is always in good shape.

As you have written only a few lines of code since the last refactor step, the changes needed to make the code clean shouldn't take much time.

TDD in Xcode

In 1998, the Swiss company Sen:te developed **OCUnit**, a testing framework for Objective-C (hence, the OC prefix). OCUnit was a port of **SUnit**, a testing framework that Kent Beck had written for Smalltalk in 1994.

With Xcode 2.1, Apple added OCUnit to Xcode. One reason for this step was that they used it to develop **Core Data** at the same time that they developed **Tiger**, the OS with which Core Data was shipped. Bill Bumgarner, an Apple engineer, wrote this later in a blog post:

> *"Core Data 1.0 is not perfect, but it is a rock solid product that I'm damned proud of. The quality and performance achieved could not have been done without the use of unit testing. Furthermore, we were able to perform highly disruptive operations to the codebase very late in the development cycle. The end result was a vast increase in performance, a much cleaner codebase, and rock solid release."*

Apple realized how valuable unit tests can be when developing complex systems in a changing environment. They wanted third-party developers to benefit from unit tests as well. OCUnit could be (and has been) added to Xcode by hand before version 2.1. But by including it into the IDE, the investment in time that was needed to start unit testing was reduced a lot, and as a result, more people started to write tests.

In 2008, OCUnit was integrated into the iPhone SDK 2.2 to allow unit testing of iPhone apps.

Finally, in 2013, unit testing became a first-class citizen in Xcode 5 with the introduction of **XCTest**. With XCTest, Apple added specific user interface elements to Xcode that helped with testing, which allowed running specific tests, finding failing tests quickly, and getting an overview of all the tests. We will go over the testing user interface in Xcode later in this chapter. But, first, we will take a look at TDD using Xcode in action.

An example of TDD

For this TDD example, we are going to use the same project we created at the beginning of this chapter. Open the `FirstDemo` project in Xcode, and run the tests by hitting *command +* U. The one existing test should pass.

Let's say we are building an app for a blogging platform. When writing a new post, the user puts in a headline for the post. All the words in the headline should start with an uppercase letter.

To start the TDD workflow, we need a failing test. The following questions need to be considered when writing the test:

- **Precondition**: What is the state of the system before we invoke the method?
- **Invocation**: How should the signature of the method look? What are the input parameters (if any) of the method?
- **Assertion**: What is the expected result of the method invocation?

For our blogging app example, here are some possible answers to these questions:

- **Precondition**: None.
- **Invocation**: The method should take a string and it should return a string. A possible name for that method is `makeHeadline`.
- **Assertion**: The resulting string should be the same, but all the words should start with an uppercase letter.

This is enough to get us started. Enter the red step.

Red - example 1

Open `FirstDemoTests.swift`, and add the following code to the `FirstDemoTests` class:

```
func test_MakeHeadline_ReturnsStringWithEachWordStartCapital() {
    let viewController = ViewController()

    let string = "this is A test headline"

    let headline = viewController.makeHeadline(from: string)
}
```

This isn't a complete test method yet because we aren't really testing anything. The assertion is missing. But we have to stop writing the test at this point because the compiler complains that `Value of type 'ViewController' has no member 'makeHeadline'`.

Following the TDD workflow, we need to add code until the compiler stops printing errors. Remember that *code does not compile* within a test means *the test is failing*. And a failing test means we need to write code until the test does not fail anymore.

Open `ViewController.swift`, and add the following method to the `ViewController` class:

```
func makeHeadline(from string: String) {
}
```

The error still remains. The reason for this is that we need to compile to make the test target aware of this change. Run the tests to check whether this change is enough to make the test green again. The test is indeed green, but sometimes the error is still shown. The reason is that Xcode sometimes "forgets" to remove old errors.

Now we get a warning that the headline constant isn't used, and we should change it to _. So, let's use it. Add the following assert function at the end of the test:

```
XCTAssertEqual(headline, "This Is A Test Headline")
```

This results in another compiler error:

`Argument type '()' does not conform to expected type 'Equatable'`

The reason for this error is that the `makeHeadline(from:)` method at the moment returns `Void` or `()`. But `XCTAssertEqual` can only be used if both expressions conform to the protocol `Equatable` and are of the same type. This makes sense as two expressions of different types can't be equal to each other.

Go back to `ViewController`, and change `makeHeadline(from:)` to this:

```
func makeHeadline(from string: String) -> String {
    return ""
}
```

Green - example 1

Now, the method returns an empty string. This should be enough to make the test compile. Run the test. The test fails. But this time, it's not because the code we've written does not compile, but due to the failed assertion instead. This is not a surprise because an empty string isn't equal to "This Is A Test Headline". Following the TDD workflow, we need to go back to the implementation and add the simplest code that makes the test pass.

In `ViewController`, change `makeHeadline(from:)` to read as follows:

```
func makeHeadline(from string: String) -> String {
   return "This Is A Test Headline"
}
```

This code is stupid and wrong, but it is the simplest code that makes the test pass. Run the tests to make sure that this is actually the case.

Even though the code we just wrote is useless for the feature we are trying to implement, it still has value for us, the developers. It tells us that we need another test.

Refactor - example 1

Before writing more tests, we need to refactor the existing ones. In the production code, there is nothing to refactor. This code couldn't be simpler or more elegant. In the test case, we now have two test methods. Both start by creating an instance of `ViewController`. This is a repetition of code and a good candidate for refactoring.

Add the following property at the beginning of the `FirstDemoTests` class:

```
var viewController: ViewController!
```

Remember that the `setUp()` method is called before each test is executed. So, it is the perfect place to initialize the `viewController` property:

```
override func setUp() {
   super.setUp()
   viewController = ViewController()
}
```

Now, we can remove this `let viewController = ViewController()` line of code from each test.

Red - example 2

As mentioned in the preceding section, we need another test because the production code we have written to make the previous test pass only works for one specific headline. But the feature we want to implement has to work for all possible headlines. Add the following test to `FirstDemoTests`:

```
func test_MakeHeadline_ReturnsStringWithEachWordStartCapital2() {
    let string = "Here is another Example"

    let headline = viewController.makeHeadline(from: string)

    XCTAssertEqual(headline, "Here Is Another Example")
}
```

Run the test. This new test obviously fails. Let's make the tests green.

Green - example 2

Open `ViewController.swift`, and replace the implementation of `makeHeadline(from:)` with the following lines of code:

```
func makeHeadline(from string: String) -> String {
    let words = string.components(separatedBy: " ")

    var headline = ""
    for var word in words {
      let firstCharacter = word.remove(at: word.startIndex)
      headline += "\(String(firstCharacter).uppercased())\(word) "
    }
    headline.remove(at: headline.index(before: headline.endIndex))
    return headline
}
```

Let's go through this implementation step by step:

1. Split the string into words.
2. Iterate over the words, and remove the first character and change it to uppercase. Add the changed character to the beginning of the word. Add this word with a trailing space to the headline string.
3. Remove the last space and return the string.

Run the tests. All the tests pass. The next thing to perform in the TDD workflow is refactoring.

 Do not skip refactoring. This step is as important as the red and the green step. You are not done until there is nothing to refactor anymore.

Refactor - example 2

Look at the two tests you have for this feature. They are hard to read. The relevant information for the tests is kind of unstructured. We are going to clean it up.

Replace the two tests with the following code:

```
func test_MakeHeadline_ReturnsStringWithEachWordStartCapital() {
    let input          = "this is A test headline"
    let expectedOutput = "This Is A Test Headline"

    let headline = viewController.makeHeadline(from: input)

    XCTAssertEqual(headline, expectedOutput)
}

func test_MakeHeadline_ReturnsStringWithEachWordStartCapital2() {
    let input          = "Here is another Example"
    let expectedOutput = "Here Is Another Example"

    let headline = viewController.makeHeadline(from: input)

    XCTAssertEqual(headline, expectedOutput)
}
```

Now, the tests are easy to read and understand. They follow a logical structure: precondition, invocation, and assertion.

Run the tests. All the tests should still pass. But how do we know whether the tests still test the same thing as they did earlier? In most cases, the changes we'll make while refactoring the tests don't need to be tested themselves. But, sometimes (such as in this case), it is good to make sure that the tests still work. This means that we need a failing test again. Go to `makeHeadline(from:)` and comment out (by adding `//` at the beginning) the line:

```
headline.remove(at: headline.index(before: headline.endIndex))
```

Run the tests again. Eureka! Both tests fail.

As you can see here, a failing test does not stop the tests in general. But you can change this behavior by setting `continueAfterFailure` to `false` in `setUp()`.

Remove the comment symbols again to make the test pass again. Now, we need to refactor the implementation code. The implementation we have right now looks like it was translated from Objective-C to Swift (if you haven't used Objective-C yet, you have to trust me on this). But Swift is different and has many concepts that make it possible to write less code that is easier to read. Let's make the implementation more swiftly. Replace `makeHeadline(from:)` with the following code:

```
func makeHeadline(from string: String) -> String {
    let words = string.components(separatedBy: " ")

    let headlineWords = words.map { (word) -> String in
        var mutableWord = word
        let first = mutableWord.remove(at: mutableWord.startIndex)

        return String(first).uppercased() + mutableWord
        }

    return headlineWords.joined(separator: " ")
}
```

In this implementation, we use the `map` function to iterate the `words` array and return another array containing the same words, but starting with uppercase letters. The result is then transformed into a string by joining the `words` using a space as the separator.

Run the tests again to make sure we didn't break anything with the refactoring. All the tests should still pass.

A recap

In this section, we have added a feature to our project using the TDD workflow. We started with a failing test. We made the test pass. And, finally, we refactored the code to be clean. The steps you have seen here seem so simple and stupid that you may think that you could skip some of the tests and still be good. But then, it's not TDD anymore. The beauty of TDD is that the steps are so easy that you do not have to think about them. You just have to remember what the next step is.

Because the steps and the rules are so easy, you don't have to waste your brainpower thinking about what the steps actually mean. The only thing you have to remember is red, green, and refactor. As a result, you can concentrate on the difficult part: writing tests, making them pass, and improving code.

Finding information about tests in Xcode

With Xcode 5 and the introduction of XCTest, unit testing became tightly integrated into Xcode. Apple added many UI elements to navigate to tests, run specific tests, and find information about failing tests. One key element here is the **Test Navigator**.

Test Navigator

To open the Test Navigator, click on the diamond with a minus sign (-) in the navigator panel:

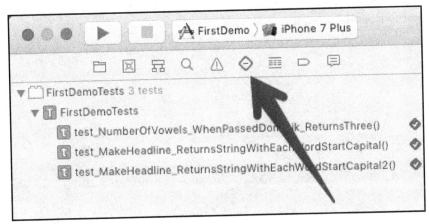

The Test Navigator shows all the tests. In the preceding screenshot, you can see the Test Navigator for our demo project. In the project, there is one test target. For complex apps, it can be useful to have more than one test target, but this is beyond the scope of this book. The number of tests is shown right behind the name of the test target. In our case, there are three tests in the target.

The demo project has only one test case with three tests.

At the bottom of the navigator is a filter control with which you can filter the shown tests. As soon as you start typing, the shown tests are filtered using fuzzy matching. There's a button in the control showing a diamond with an **x**:

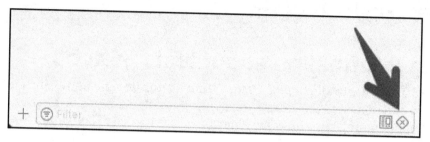

If this button is clicked on, only the failing tests are shown in the list.

Tests overview

Xcode also has a test overview where all the results of the tests are collected in one place. To open it, select the **Result Navigator** in the navigator panel, and select the last test in the list:

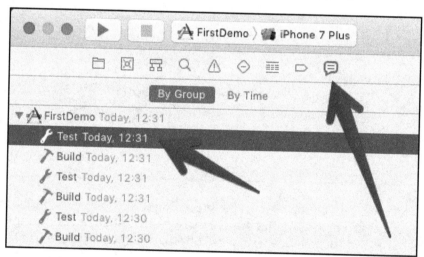

You can also select other tests in the list if you want to compare test runs with each other. In the editor on the right-hand side, an overview of all the tests from the selected test run is shown:

When you hover over one of the tests with the mouse pointer, a circle with an arrow to the right appears. If you click on the arrow, Xcode opens the test in the editor.

In the overview, there is also the **Logs** tab. It shows all the tests in a tree-like structure. Here is an example of what this looks like:

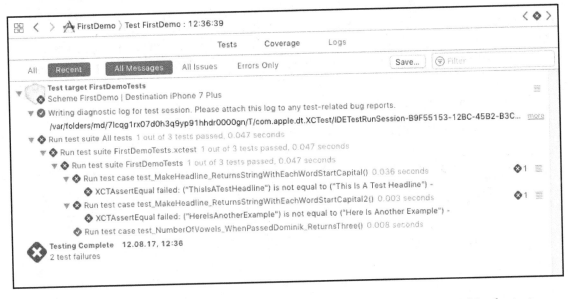

The logs show the test cases (in this example, one test case) and the tests within the test cases (in this example, two failing and one passing test). And in addition to this, the time each test case and even each test need to execute.

In TDD, it is important for the tests to execute quickly. You want to be able to execute the whole test suite in less than a second. Otherwise, the whole workflow is dominated by test execution and testing can distract your focus and concentration. You should never be tempted to switch to another application (such as Safari) because the tests will take half a minute.

If you notice that the test suite takes too long to be practical, open the logs and search for the tests that slow down testing and try to make the tests faster.

Running tests

Xcode provides many different ways to execute tests. You have already seen two ways to execute all the tests in the test suite--go to the **Project | Test** menu item and use the *command + U* keyboard shortcut.

Running one specific test

In TDD, you normally want to run all the tests as often as possible. Running the tests gives you confidence that the code does what you intended when you wrote the tests. In addition to this, you want immediate feedback (that is, a failing test) whenever new code breaks a seemingly unrelated feature. Immediate feedback means that your memory of the changes that broke the feature is fresh, and the fix is made quickly.

Nevertheless, sometimes, you need to run one specific test, but don't let it become a habit.

To run one specific test, you can click on the diamond visible next to the test method:

```
      func test_MakeHeadline_ReturnsStringWithEachWordStartCapital2() {
58        let input          = "Here is another Example"
59          expectedOutput = "Here Is Another Example"
60
61
62      let headlin  = viewController.makeHeadline(from: input)
63
64
65      XCTAssertEqual(headline, expectedOutput)
66    }
```

When you click on it, the production code is compiled and launched in the simulator or on the device, and the test is executed.

There is another way to execute exactly one specific test. When you open the Test Navigator and hover over one test, a circle with a play icon is shown next to the test method name:

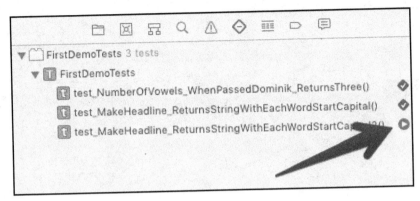

Again, if you click on this test, it is run exclusively.

The test framework identifies tests by the prefix of the method name. If you want to run all tests but one, remove the `test` prefix from the beginning of this test method name.

Running all tests in a test case

In the same way as running one specific test, you can run all the tests of a specific test case. Click on the diamond next to the definition of the test case, or click on the **Play** button that appears when you hover over the test case name in the Test Navigator.

Running a group of tests

You can choose to run a group of tests by editing the build scheme. To edit the build scheme, click on the scheme in the toolbar in Xcode, and then click on **Edit Scheme...**:

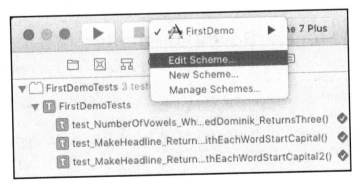

Then, select **Test**, and expand the test suite by clicking on the small triangle. On the right-hand side, there is a column called **Test**:

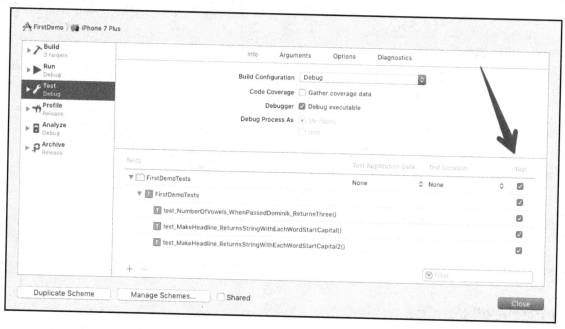

The selected scheme only runs the tests that are checked. By default, all the tests are checked, but you can uncheck some tests if you need to. But don't forget to check all the tests again when you are finished.

As an alternative, you can add a build scheme for a group of tests that you want to run regularly without running all tests.

But as mentioned earlier, you should run the complete test suite as often as possible.

The setUp() and tearDown() methods

We have already seen the setUp() and tearDown() instance methods earlier in this chapter. The code in the setUp() instance method is run before each test invocation. In our example, we used setUp() to initialize ViewController that we wanted to test. As it was run before each test invocation, each test used its own instance of ViewController. The changes we made to this particular instance in one test didn't affect the other test. The tests executed independently of each other.

The `tearDown()` instance method is run after each test invocation. Use `tearDown()` to perform the necessary cleanup.

In addition to the instance methods, there are also the `setUp()` and `tearDown()` class methods. These are run before and after all the tests of a test case, respectively.

Debugging tests

Sometimes, but usually, rarely, you may need to debug your tests. As with normal code, you can set breakpoints in test code. The debugger then stops the execution of the code at a breakpoint. You can also set breakpoints in the code that will be tested to check whether you have missed something or whether the code you'd like to test is actually executed.

To get a feeling of how this works, let's add an error to a test in the preceding example and debug it. Open `FirstDemoTests.swift`, and replace the `test_MakeHeadline_ReturnsStringWithEachWordStartCapital2()` test method with this code:

```
func test_MakeHeadline_ReturnsStringWithEachWordStartCapital2() {
    let input           = "Here is another Example"
    let expectedOutput  = "Here iS Another Example"

    let headline = viewController.makeHeadline(from: input)

    XCTAssertEqual(headline, expectedOutput)
}
```

Have you seen the error that we have introduced? The value of the string `expectedOutput` has a typo. The letter s in `iS` is an uppercase letter, and the letter i is a lowercase letter. Run the tests. The test fails and Xcode tells you what the problem is. But for the sake of this exercise, let's set a breakpoint in the line with the `XCTAssertEqual()` function. Click on the area on the left-hand side of the line where you want to set a breakpoint. You have to click on the area next to the red diamond.

As a result, your editor will look similar to what is shown here:

```
     func test_MakeHeadline_ReturnsStringWithEachWordStartCapital2() {
58       let input         = "Here is another Example"
59       let expectedOutput = "Here iS Another Example"
60
61
62       let headline = viewController.makeHeadline(from: input)
63
64
65       XCTAssertEqual(headline, expectedOutput)   ⬥ XCTAssertEqual failed: ("Here Is Another Exam...
66     } |
```

Run the tests again. The execution of the tests stops at the breakpoint. Open the debug console if it is not already open (go to **View** | **Debug Area** | **Activate Console**). In the console, some test output is visible. The last line starts with (lldb) and a blinking cursor. Put in po expectedOutput and hit return. po is the "print object" command. As the name suggests, it prints a representation of the object:

```
(lldb) po expectedOutput
"Here iS Another Example"
```

Now, print the value of the result:

```
(lldb) po headline
"Here Is Another Example"
```

So, with the help of the debugger, you can find out what is happening.

 To learn more about the debugger, search for lldb in the Apple documentation.

For now, keep the typo in expectedOutput as it is, but remove the breakpoint by dragging it with the mouse from the area to the left of the editor.

Breakpoint that breaks on test failure

Xcode has a built-in breakpoint that breaks on test failures. When this breakpoint is set, the execution of the tests is stopped, and a debug session is started whenever a test fails.

Usually, this is not what you want because in TDD failing tests are normal, and you don't need a debugger to find out what's going on. You explicitly wrote the test to fail at the beginning of the TDD workflow cycle.

But in case you need to debug one or more failing tests, it's good to know how this breakpoint is activated. Open the Debug Navigator:

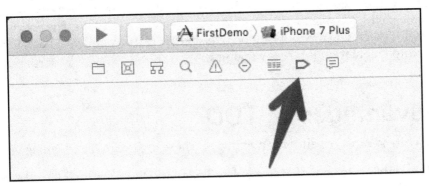

At the bottom of the navigator view is a button with a plus sign (+). Click on it, and select **Test Failure Breakpoint**:

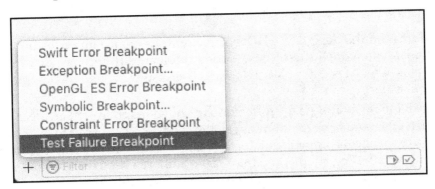

As the name suggests, this breakpoint stops the execution of the tests whenever a test fails. We still have a failing test in our example. Run the tests to see the breakpoint in action.

The debugger stops at the line with the assertion because the tests fail. Like in the preceding example, you get a debug session so that you can put in LLDB commands to find out why the test failed.

Remove the breakpoint again because it's not very practical while performing TDD.

The test again feature

Now, let's fix the error in the tests and learn how to run the previous test again. Open `FirstDemoTests.swift`, and run only the failing test by clicking on the diamond symbol next to the test method. The test still fails. Fix it by changing `iS` to `Is` in `expectedOutput`. Then, go to **Product | Perform Action | Test "test_MakeHeadline_ReturnsStringWithEachWordStartCapital2()" Again**, or use the shortcut *ctrl + option + command + G* to run just the previous test again. The shortcut is especially useful when you are working on one specific feature, and you need to test whether the implementation is already enough.

The advantages of TDD

TDD comes with advantages and disadvantages. These are the main advantages:

- **You only write code that is needed**: Following the rules, you have to stop writing production code when all your tests pass. If your project needs another feature, you need a test to drive the implementation of that feature. The code you write is the simplest code possible. So, all the code ending up in the product is actually needed to implement the features.

- **More modular design**: In TDD, you concentrate on one micro feature at a time. And as you write the test first, the code automatically becomes easy to test. Code that is easy to test has a clear interface. This results in a modular design for your application.

- **Easier to maintain**: As the different parts of your application are decoupled from each other and have clear interfaces, the code becomes easier to maintain. You can exchange the implementation of a micro feature with a better implementation without affecting another module. You could even keep the tests and rewrite the complete application. When all the tests pass, you are done.

- **Easier to refactor**: Every feature is thoroughly tested. You don't need to be afraid to make drastic changes because if all the tests still pass, everything is fine. This point is very important because you, as a developer, improve your skills each and every day. If you open the project after six months of working on something else, most probably, you'll have many ideas on how to improve the code. But your memory about all the different parts and how they fit together isn't fresh anymore. So, making changes can be dangerous. With a complete test suite, you can easily improve the code without the fear of breaking your application.

- **High test coverage**: There is a test for every feature. This results in high test coverage. High test coverage helps you gain confidence in your code.
- **Tests document the code**: The test code shows you how your code is meant to be used. As such, it documents your code. The test code is sample code that shows what the code does and how the interface has to be used.
- **Less debugging**: How often have you wasted a day to find a nasty bug? How often have you copied an error message from Xcode and searched for it on the internet? With TDD, you write fewer bugs because the tests tell you early on whether you've made a mistake. And the bugs you write are found much earlier. You can concentrate on fixing the bug when your memory about what the code is supposed to do and how it does it.

The disadvantages of TDD

Just like everything else in the world, TDD has some disadvantages. The main ones are here:

- **No silver bullet**: Tests help to find bugs, but they can't find bugs that you introduce in the test code and in implementation code. If you haven't understood the problem you need to solve, writing tests most probably won't help.

- **It seems slower at the beginning**: If you start TDD, you will get the feeling that it takes longer to make easy implementations. You need to think about the interfaces, write the test code, and run the tests before you can finally start writing the code.
- **All the members of a team need to do it**: As TDD influences the design of code, it is recommended that either all the members of a team use TDD or no one at all. In addition to this, it's sometimes difficult to justify TDD to the management because they often have the feeling that the implementation of new features takes longer if developers write code that won't end up in the product half of the time. It helps if the whole team agrees on the importance of unit tests.
- **Tests need to be maintained when requirements change**: Probably, the strongest argument against TDD is that the tests have to be maintained as the code has to. Whenever requirements change, you need to change the code and tests. But you are working with TDD. This means that you need to change the tests first, and then make the tests pass. So, in reality, tests help you to understand the new requirements and implement the code without breaking other features.

What to test

What should be tested? When using TDD and following the rules mentioned in the previous sections, the answer is easy--everything. You only write code because there is a failing test.

In practice, it's not that easy. For example, should the position and color of a button be tested? Should the view hierarchy be tested? Probably not; the color and exact position of the button is not important for the functioning of an app. In the early stages of development, these kinds of things tend to change. With the auto layout and different localizations of the app, the exact position of buttons and labels depend on many parameters.

In general, you should test the features that make the app useful for a user and those that need to work. The user doesn't care whether the button is exactly 20 points from the rightmost edge of the screen. All the user is interested in is that the button does what they expect it to and the app looks good.

In addition to this, you should not test the whole application in total using unit tests. Unit tests are meant to test small units of computation. They need to be fast and reliable. Things, such as database access and networking, should be tested using integration tests, where the tests drive the real finished application. Integration tests are allowed to be slow because they are run a lot less often than unit tests. Usually, they are run at the end of the development before the application is released, or they are run with the help of a continuous integration system each night on a server, where it doesn't matter that the complete test suite takes several minutes (or even hours) to execute.

Summary

In this chapter, we saw unit tests in action and how they are set up in Xcode. You learned what TDD is and why it can help build better apps. With the help of TDD, we implemented a feature of a demo app to get used to the workflow. We saw many different possibilities to run tests and how we can find bugs in our tests using LLDB, the debugger integrated into Xcode. Finally, we discussed the advantages and disadvantages of TDD and what should be tested with unit tests.

In the next chapter, we will take a look at an app that we will build together using TDD.

2
Planning and Structuring Your Test-Driven iOS App

In the previous chapter, you learned how to write unit tests and saw an easy example of TDD. When starting TDD, writing unit tests is easy for most people. The hard part is to transfer knowledge from *writing test* to *driving development*. What can be assumed? What should be done before one writes the first test? What should be tested to end up with a complete app?

As a developer, you are used to thinking in terms of code. When you see a feature on the requirement list for an app, your brain already starts to layout the code for this feature. For recurring problems in iOS development (such as building table views), you most probably have already developed your own best practices.

In TDD, you should not think about the code while working on the test. The tests have to describe what the unit under test should do and not how it should do it. It should be possible to change the implementation without breaking the tests. Thinking like this is the hard part about TDD. You'll need a lot of practice before this becomes natural.

To practice this approach of development, we will develop a simple to-do list app in the remainder of this book. It is, on purpose, a boring and easy app. We want to concentrate on the TDD workflow, not complex implementations. An interesting app would distract from what is important in this book--how to perform TDD.

This chapter introduces the app we are going to build and shows the views that the finished app will have.

We will cover the following topics in this chapter:

- The task list view
- The task detail view
- The task input view
- The structure of an app
- Getting started with Xcode
- Setting up useful Xcode behaviors for testing

The task list view

When starting the app, the user sees a list of to-do items. The items in the list consist of a title, an optional location, and the due date. New items can be added to the list by an add (+) button, which is shown in the navigation bar of the view. The task list view will look like this:

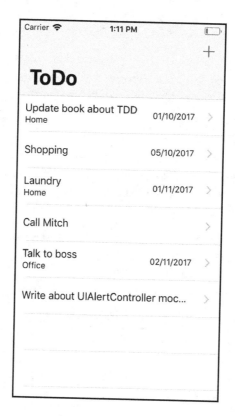

User stories:

- As a user, I want to see the list of to-do items when I open the app
- As a user, I want to add to-do items to the list

In a to-do list app, the user will obviously need to be able to check items when they are finished. The checked items are shown below the unchecked items, and it is possible to uncheck them again. The app uses the *Delete* button in the UI of UITableView to check and uncheck items. Checked items will be put at the end of the list in a section with the **Finished** header. The user can also delete all the items from the list by tapping the **Trash** button. The UI for the to-do item list will look like this:

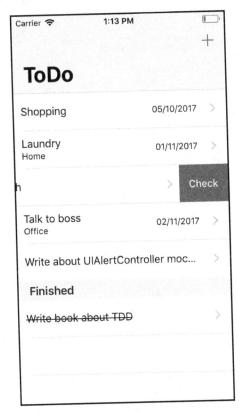

User stories:

- As a user, I want to check a to-do item to mark it as finished
- As a user, I want to see all the checked items following the unchecked items

- As a user, I want to uncheck a to-do item
- As a user, I want to delete all the to-do items

When the user taps an entry, the details of this entry are shown in the task detail view.

The task detail view

The task detail view shows all the information that's stored for a to-do item. The information consists of a title, due date, location (name and address), and a description. If an address is given, a map with an address is shown. The detail view also allows checking the item as finished. The detail view looks like this:

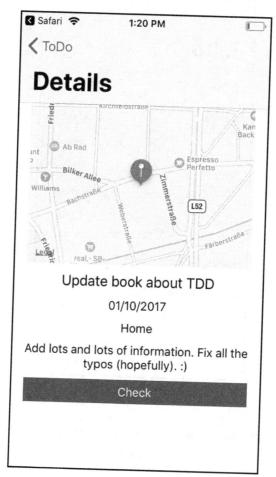

User stories:

- As a user, given that I have tapped a to-do item in the list, I want to see its details
- As a user, I want to check a to-do item from its details view

The task input view

When the user selects the add (+) button in the list view, the task input view is shown. The user can add information for the task. Only the title is required. The **Save** button can only be selected when a title is given. It is not possible to add a task that is already on the list. The **Cancel** button dismisses the view. The task input view will look like this:

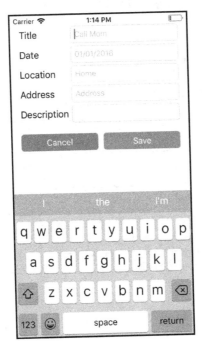

User stories:

- As a user, given that I tapped the add (+) button in the item list, I want to see a form to put in the details (title, optional date, optional location name, optional address, and optional description) of a to-do item
- As a user, I want to add a to-do item to the list of to-do items by tapping on the **Save** button

We will not implement the editing and deletion of tasks. But, when you have worked through this book completely, it will be easy for you to add this feature yourself by writing the tests first.

Keep in mind that we will not test the look and design of the app. Unit tests cannot figure out whether an app looks like it was intended. Unit tests can test features, and these are independent of their presentation. In principle, it would be possible to write unit tests for the position and color of UI elements. But, such things are very likely to change a lot in the early stages of development. We do not want to have failing tests only because a button has moved ten points.

However, we will test whether the UI elements are present in the view. If your user cannot see the information for the tasks, or if it is not possible to add all the information of a task, then the app does not meet the requirements.

The structure of the app

The following diagram shows the structure of the app:

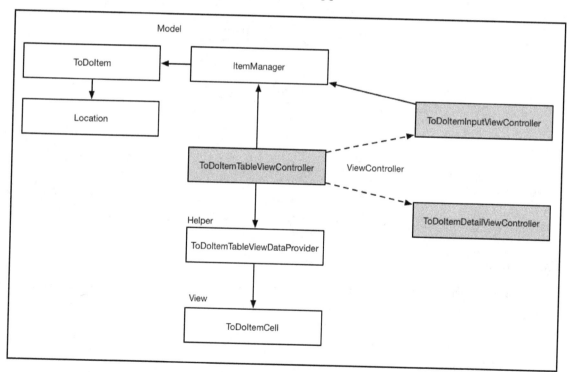

The table view controller, the delegate, and the data source

In iOS apps, data is often presented using a table view. Table views are highly optimized for performance; they are easy to use and to implement. We will use a table view for the list of to-do items.

A table view is usually represented by `UITableViewController`, which is also the data source and delegate for the table view. This often leads to a massive table view controller, because it is doing too much: presenting the view, navigating to other view controllers, and managing the presentation of the data in the table view.

Sometimes, it's a good idea to split up the responsibility into several classes. Therefore, we will use a helper class to act as the data source and delegate for the table view. The communication between the table view controller and the helper class will be defined using a protocol. Protocols define what the interface of a class looks like. This has a great benefit: if we need to replace an implementation with a better version (maybe because you have learned how to implement the feature in a better way), we only need to develop against the clear interface. The inner workings of other classes do not matter.

Table view cells

As you can see in the preceding screenshots, the to-do list items have a title and, optionally, they can have a due date and a location name. The table view cells should only show the set data. We will accomplish this by implementing our own custom table view cell.

The model

The model of the application consists of the to-do item, the location, and an item manager, which allows the addition and removal of items and is also responsible for managing the items. Therefore, the controller will ask the item manager for the items to present. The item manager will also be responsible for storing the items on the disc.

Beginners often tend to manage the model objects within the controller. Then, the controller has a reference to a collection of items, and the addition and removal of items are directly done by the controller. This is not recommended because if we decide to change the storage of the items (for example, using core data), their addition and removal would have to be changed within the controller. It is difficult to keep an overview of such a class; because of this reason, it is a source of bugs.

It's much easier to have a clear interface between the controller and the model objects because if we need to change how the model objects are managed, the controller can stay the same. We could even replace the complete model layer if we just keep the interface the same. Later in the book, we will see that this decoupling also helps to make testing easier.

Other view controllers

The application will have two more view controllers: a task detail view controller and a view controller for the input of the task.

When the user taps a to-do item in the list, the details of the item are presented in the task detail view controller. From the **Details** screen, the user will be able to check an item.

New to-do items will be added to the list of items using the view presented by the input view controller.

The development strategy

In this book, we will build the app from inside out. We will start with the model and then build the controllers and networking. At the end of the book, we will put everything together.

Usually, you would rather build apps feature-by-feature when doing TDD. But, by separating on the basis of layers instead of features, it is easier to follow and keep an overview of what is happening. When you later need to refresh your memory, the relevant information you need is easier to find.

Getting started with Xcode

Now, let's start our journey by creating a project that we will implement using TDD.

Open Xcode and create a new iOS project using the **Single View Application** template. In the options window, add ToDo as the product name, select **Swift** as language, and check the box next to **Include Unit Tests**. Let the **Use Core Data** and **Include UI Tests** boxes stay unchecked.

Xcode creates a small iOS project with two targets: one for the implementation code and the other for the unit tests. The template contains code that presents a single view on screen. We could have chosen to start with the master-detail application template because the app will show a master and a detail view. However, we have chosen the **Single View Application** template because it comes with hardly any code. In TDD, we want to have all the implementation code demanded by failing tests.

To take a look at how the application target and test target fit together, select the project in the Project Navigator, and then select the **ToDoTests** target. In the **General** tab, you'll find a setting for the **Host Application** that the test target should be able to test. It looks like this:

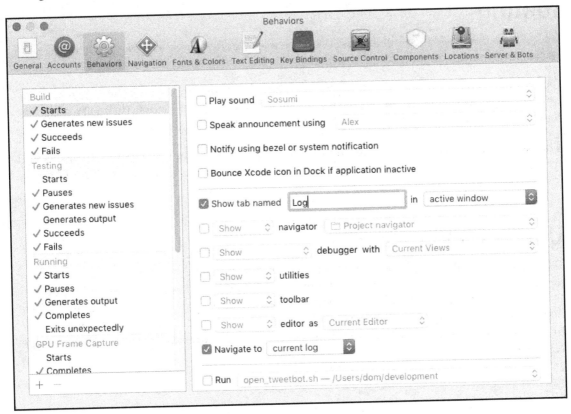

Xcode has already set up the test target correctly to allow the testing of the implementations that we will write to the application target.

Xcode has also set up a scheme to build the app and run the tests. Click on the scheme selector next to the Stop button in the toolbar, and select **Edit Scheme....** In the test action, all the test bundles of the project will be listed. In our case, only one test bundle is shown-- **ToDoTests**. On the right-hand side of the shown window is a column named **Test**, with a checked checkbox. This means that if we run the tests while this scheme is selected in Xcode, all the tests in the selected test suite will be run.

Setting up useful Xcode behaviors for testing

Xcode has a feature called **behaviors**. With the use of behaviors and tabs, Xcode can show useful information depending on its state.

Open the **Behaviors** window by navigating to **Xcode | Behaviors | Edit Behaviors**. On the left-hand side are the different stages for which you can add behaviors (**Build, Testing, Running,** and so on). The following behaviors are useful when doing TDD.

The behaviors shown here are those that I find useful. Play around with the settings to find the ones most useful for you. Overall, I recommend using behaviors because I think they speed up development.

Useful build behaviors

When the building starts, Xcode compiles the files and links them together. To see what is going on, you can activate the build log when building starts. It is recommended that you open the build log in a new tab because this allows switching back to the code editor when no error occurs during the build. Select the **Starts** stage and check **Show tab named**. Put in the Log name and select **in** as **active window**. Check the **Show navigator** setting and **Issue Navigator**.

At the bottom of the window, check **Navigate to** and select **current log**. After you have made these changes, the settings window will look like this:

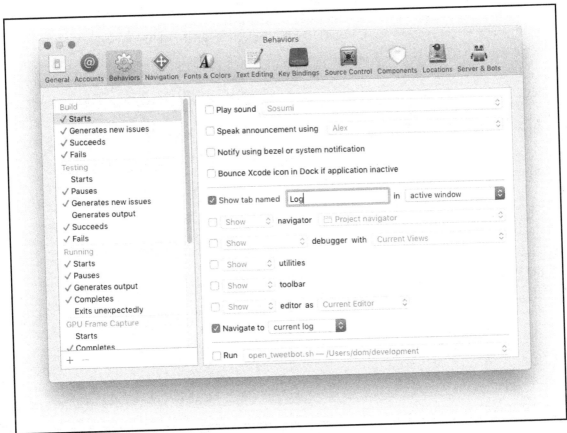

Build and run to see what the behavior looks like.

Testing behaviors

To write some code, I have an Xcode tab called **Coding**. Usually, in this tab, the test is open on the left-hand side, and in the Assistant Editor, which is on the right-hand side; there is the code to be tested (or in the case of TDD, the code to be written). It looks like the following:

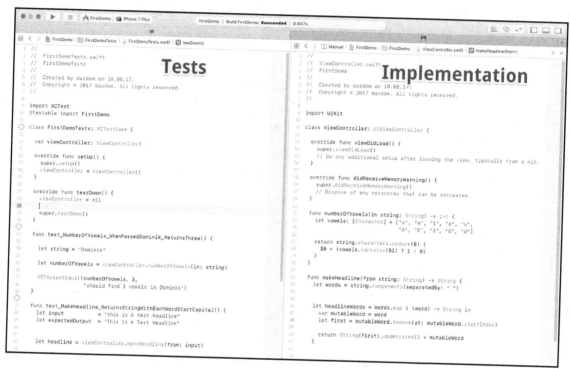

When the test starts, we want to see the code editor again. So, we add a behavior to show the **Coding** tab. In addition to this, we want to see the Test Navigator and debugger with the console view.

When the test succeeds, Xcode should show a bezel to notify us that all tests have passed. Navigate to the **Testing | Succeeds** stage and check the **Notify using bezel or system notification** setting. In addition to this, it should hide the navigator and the debugger, because we want to concentrate on refactoring or writing the next test.

In case the testing fails (which happens a lot in TDD), Xcode should show a bezel again. I like to hide the debugger, because usually, it is not the best place to figure out what is going on in the case of a failing test. In most of the cases in TDD, we already know what the problem is.

You can even make your Mac speak the announcements. Check **Speak announcements using** and select the voice you like, but be careful not to annoy your coworkers. You might need their help in the future.

Now, the project and Xcode are set up, and we can start our TDD journey.

Summary

In this chapter, we took a look at the app that we are going to build throughout the course of this book. We took a look at how the screens of the app will look when we are finished with it. We created the project that we will use later on and learned about Xcode behaviors.

In the next chapter, we will develop the data model of the app using TDD. We will use structs for the model wherever we can, because models are best represented in Swift by value types. We will add some conformance to the Equatable protocol to make the comparison of the model instances easier.

3
A Test-Driven Data Model

iOS apps are often developed using a design pattern called **Model-View-Controller** (**MVC**). In this pattern, each class, struct, or enum is either a model object, view, or a controller. Model objects are responsible for storing data. They should be independent of the kind of presentation by the UI. For example, it should be possible to use the same model object for an iOS app and a command-line tool on macOS.

View objects are the presenters of the data. They are responsible for making the objects visible (or hearable in the case of a VoiceOver-enabled app) for the user. Views are special for the device that the app is executed on. In the case of a cross-platform application, view objects cannot be shared. Each platform needs its own implementation of a view layer.

Controller objects communicate between the model and view objects. They are responsible for making the model objects presentable.

We will use MVC for our to-do app because it is one of the easiest design patterns, and it is commonly used by Apple in its sample code.

This chapter starts our journey in the field of TDD with the model layer of our application. It is divided into three sections:

- Implementing the `ToDoItem` struct
- Implementing the `Location` struct
- Implementing the `ItemManager` class

Implementing the ToDoItem struct

A to-do app needs a model class/struct to store information for to-do items.

We start by adding a new test case to the test target. Open the to-do project that we have created in the *Getting started with Xcode* section of Chapter 2, *Planning and Structuring Your Test-Driven iOS App*, and select the ToDoTests group. Go to **File | New | File...**, navigate to **iOS | Source | Unit Test Case Class**, and click on **Next**. Put in the name ToDoItemTests, make it a subclass of XCTestCase, select **Swift** as the language, and click on **Next**. In the next window click on **Create**.

Now, delete the ToDoTests.swift template test case.

At the time of writing, if you delete ToDoTests.swift before you add the first test case in a test target, you will see a pop-up from Xcode telling you that adding the Swift file will create a mixed Swift and Objective-C target:

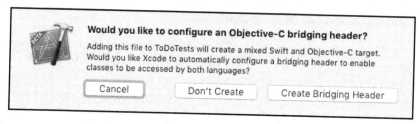

 This is a bug in Xcode 9.0. It seems that when you add the first Swift file to a target, Xcode assumes that there have to be Objective-C files already. Click on **Don't Create** if this happens to you because we will not use Objective-C in our tests.

Adding a title property

Open ToDoItemTests.swift and add the following import expression right below import XCTest:

```
@testable import ToDo
```

This is needed in order to be able to test the ToDo module. The @testable keyword makes the internal methods of the ToDo module accessible to the test case.

Remove the two template test methods, testExample() and testPerformanceExample().

The title of a to-do item is required. Let's write a test to ensure that an initializer exists that will take a `title` string. Add the following test method to the end of the test case (but within the `ToDoItemTests` class):

```
func test_Init_TakesTitle() {
    ToDoItem(title: "Foo")
}
```

The static analyzer built into Xcode will complain about `Use of unresolved identifier 'ToDoItem'`:

```
       func test_Init_TakesTitle() {
25         ToDoItem(title: "Foo")                    ● Use of unresolved identifier 'ToDoItem'
26     }
```

We cannot compile this code because Xcode cannot find the `ToDoItem` identifier. Remember that a non-compiling test is a failing test; and as soon as we have a failing test, we need to write implementation code to make the test pass.

To add a file for the implementation code, first, click on the `ToDo` group in the Project Navigator. Otherwise, the added file will be put into the test group. Go to **File | New | File...**, navigate to the **iOS | Source | Swift File** template, and click on **Next**. In the **Save As** field, add the name `ToDoItem.swift`; make sure that the file is added to the `ToDo` target and not to the `ToDoTests` target, and click on **Create**.

Open `ToDoItem.swift` in the editor, and add the following code:

```
struct ToDoItem {
}
```

This code is a complete implementation of a struct named `ToDoItem`. So, Xcode should now be able to find the `ToDoItem` identifier. Run the test by either going to **Product | Test** or using the *command + U* shortcut. The code does not compile because there is an argument passed to a call that takes no arguments. This means that at this stage, we could initialize an instance of `ToDoItem` like this:

```
let item = ToDoItem()
```

But we want to have an initializer that takes a title. We need to add a property, named `title`, of type `String` to store the title:

```
struct ToDoItem {
    let title: String
}
```

Run the test again. It will pass. We have implemented the first micro feature of our to-do app using TDD. And it wasn't even hard. For the rest of the book, we will do this over and over again until the app is finished. But we first need to check whether there is anything to refactor in the existing test and implementation code. The tests and code are clean and simple. There is nothing to refactor yet.

 Always remember to check whether refactoring is needed after you have made the tests green.

There are, however, a few things to note about the test. First, Xcode shows a `Result of 'ToDoItem' initializer is unused` warning. To make this warning go away, assign the result of the initializer to an underscore `_ = ToDoItem(title: "Foo")`. This tells Xcode that we know what we are doing. We want to call the initializer of `ToDoItem`, but we do not care about its return value.

Second, there is no `XCTAssert` function call in the test. To add an assert, we could rewrite the test like this:

```
func test_Init_TakesTitle() {
    let item = ToDoItem(title: "Foo")
    XCTAssertNotNil(item, "item should not be nil")
}
```

But in Swift, a non-failable initializer cannot return `nil`. It always returns a valid instance. This means that the `XCTAssertNotNil()` method is useless. We do not need it to ensure that we have written enough code to implement the tested micro feature. Following the rules of TDD mentioned in `Chapter 1`, *Your First Unit Tests*, we are not allowed to write this code. It is not needed to drive the development, and it does not make the code better.

Before we proceed with the next few tests, let's set up the editor in a way that makes the TDD workflow easier and faster. Open `ToDoItemTests.swift` in the editor. Open Project Navigator, and hold down the *Option* key while clicking on `ToDoItem.swift` in the navigator to open it in the Assistant Editor. Depending on the size of your screen and your preferences, you might prefer to hide the navigator again. With this setup, you have the tests and the code side by side, and switching from test to code and vice versa takes no time. In addition to this, as the relevant test is visible while you write the code, it can guide the implementation.

Adding an itemDescription property

A to-do item can have a description. We would like to have an initializer that also takes a description string. To drive the implementation, we need a failing test for the existence of this initializer:

```
func test_Init_TakesTitleAndDescription() {
    _ = ToDoItem(title: "Foo",
                 itemDescription: "Bar")
}
```

Again, this code does not compile because there is Extra argument 'itemDescription' in call. To make this test pass, we add an itemDescription property of type String? to ToDoItem:

```
struct ToDoItem {
    let title: String
    let itemDescription: String?
}
```

Run the tests. The test_Init_TakesTitle() test fails (that is, it does not compile) because there is Missing argument for parameter 'itemDescription' in the call. The reason for this is that we use a feature of Swift where structs have an automatic initializer with arguments defining their properties. The initializer in the first test only has one argument, and therefore, the test fails. To make the two tests pass again, we need to add an initializer that can take a variable number of parameters. Swift functions (and init methods as well) can have default values for parameters. You will use this feature to set itemDescription to nil if there is no parameter for it in the initializer.

Add the following code to ToDoItem:

```
init(title: String,
     itemDescription: String? = nil) {

    self.title = title
    self.itemDescription = itemDescription
}
```

This initializer has two arguments. The second argument has a default value, so we do not need to provide both arguments. When the second argument is omitted, the default value is used.

Now, run the tests to make sure that both tests pass.

Removing a hidden source of bugs

To be able to use a short initializer only setting the title, we need to define it ourselves. But this also introduces a new source of potential bugs. We can remove the two micro features we have implemented and still have both tests pass. To take a look at how this works, open ToDoItem.swift, and comment out the properties and assignment in the initializer:

```
struct ToDoItem {
//   let title: String
//   let itemDescription: String?

    init(title: String,
         itemDescription: String? = nil) {

//      self.title = title
//      self.itemDescription = itemDescription
    }
}
```

Run the tests. Both tests still pass. The reason for this is that they do not check whether the values of the initializer arguments are actually set to any ToDoItem properties. We can easily extend the tests to make sure that the values are set. First, let's change the name of the first test to test_Init_WhenGivenTitle_SetsTitle(), and replace its contents with the following code:

```
let item = ToDoItem(title: "Foo")
XCTAssertEqual(item.title, "Foo",
               "should set title")
```

This test does not compile because ToDoItem does not have a title property (it is commented out). This shows that the test is now testing our intention. Remove the comment signs for the title property and assignment of the title in the initializer, and run the tests again. All the tests pass. Now, replace the second test with this one:

```
func test_Init_WhenGivenDescription_SetsDescription() {
    let item = ToDoItem(title: "",
                        itemDescription: "Bar")
    XCTAssertEqual(item.itemDescription, "Bar",
                   "should set itemDescription")
}
```

Remove the remaining comment signs in ToDoItem, and run the tests again. Both the tests pass again, and they now actually test that the initializer works.

It is a good idea to use speaking test method names. It's quite common to use a pattern such as `test_<method name>_<precondition>_<expected behavior>`. This way, the method name tells all that you need to know about the test when a test fails. In this book, we will try to follow this pattern, but we will leave out some information (for example, the precondition), when the code gets harder to read because of the limited space here in the book. You should develop your own pattern and use it in all your tests.

Adding a timestamp property

A `ToDoItem` can also have a due date represented by a timestamp. Add the following test to make sure we can initialize an instance of `ToDoItem` with `timestamp`:

```
func test_Init_SetsTimestamp() {
    let item = ToDoItem(title: "",
                        timestamp: 0.0)

    XCTAssertEqual(item.timestamp, 0.0,
                "should set timestamp")
}
```

Again, this test does not compile because there is an extra argument in the initializer. From the implementation of the other properties, we know that we have to add a `timestamp` property in `ToDoItem` and set it in the initializer:

```
struct ToDoItem {
    let title: String
    let itemDescription: String?
    let timestamp: Double?

    init(title: String,
         itemDescription: String? = nil,
         timestamp: Double? = nil) {
        self.title = title
        self.itemDescription = itemDescription
        self.timestamp = timestamp
    }
}
```

Run the tests. All the tests pass. The tests are green and there is nothing to refactor.

Adding a location property

The last property that we would like to be able to set in the initializer of `ToDoItem` is its location. The location has a name and can optionally have a coordinate. We will use a struct to encapsulate this data into its own type. Add the following code to `ToDoItemTests`:

```
func test_Init_WhenGivenLocation_SetsLocation() {
    let location = Location(name: "Foo")
}
```

The test is not finished, but it already fails because `Location` is an unresolved identifier. There is no class, struct, or enum named `Location` yet. Open the Project Navigator, add a Swift file with the name `Location.swift` to the `ToDo` target. From our experience with the `ToDoItem` struct, we already know what is needed to make the test green. Add the following code to `Location.swift`:

```
struct Location {
    let name: String
}
```

This defines a struct `Location` with a `name` property and makes the test code compilable again. But the test is not finished yet. Add the following code to `test_Init_SetsLocation()`:

```
func test_Init_SetsLocation() {

    let location = Location(name: "Foo")
    let item = ToDoItem(title: "",
                        location: location)

    XCTAssertEqual(item.location?.name,
                   location.name,
                   "should set location")
}
```

Unfortunately, we cannot use the `location` itself yet to check for equality, so the following assert does not work:

```
XCTAssertEqual(item.location, location,
               "should set location")
```

The reason for this is that the first two arguments of `XCTAssertEqual()` have to conform to the `Equatable` protocol. We will add the protocol conformance later in this chapter.

Again, this does not compile because the initializer of `ToDoItem` does not have an argument called `location`. Add the `location` property and initializer argument to `ToDoItem`. The result should look like this:

```
struct ToDoItem {
    let title: String
    let itemDescription: String?
    let timestamp: Double?
    let location: Location?

    init(title: String,
         itemDescription: String? = nil,
         timestamp: Double? = nil,
         location: Location? = nil) {

        self.title = title
        self.itemDescription = itemDescription
        self.timestamp = timestamp
        self.location = location
    }
}
```

Run the tests again. All the tests pass and there is nothing to refactor.

We have now implemented a struct to hold the `ToDoItem` using TDD.

Implementing the Location struct

In the previous section, we added a struct to hold information about the location. We will now add tests to make sure that `Location` has the required properties and initializer.

The tests could be added to `ToDoItemTests`, but they are easier to maintain when the test classes mirror the implementation classes/structs. So, we need a new test case class.

Open the Project Navigator, select the `ToDoTests` group, and add a unit test case class with the name `LocationTests`. Make sure that you go to **iOS** | **Source** | **Unit Test Case Class** because we want to test the iOS code, and Xcode sometimes navigates to **OS X** | **Source**.

Set up the editor to show `LocationTests.swift` on the left-hand side and `Location.swift` in the Assistant Editor on the right-hand side. In the test class, add `@testable import ToDo`, and remove the `testExample()` and `testPerformanceExample()` template tests.

Adding a coordinate property

To drive the addition of a `coordinate` property, we need a failing test. Add the following test to `LocationTests`:

```swift
func test_Init_SetsCoordinate() {
    let coordinate =
        CLLocationCoordinate2D(latitude: 1,
                               longitude: 2)

    let location = Location(name: "",
                            coordinate: coordinate)

    XCTAssertEqual(location.coordinate?.latitude,
                   coordinate.latitude)
    XCTAssertEqual(location.coordinate?.longitude,
                   coordinate.longitude)
}
```

First, we create a coordinate and use it to create an instance of `Location`. Then, we assert that the `latitude` and `longitude` of the `location` coordinates are set to the correct values. We use the values 1 and 2 in the initializer of `CLLocationCoordinate2D`, because it also has an initializer that takes no arguments (`CLLocationCoordinate2D()`) and sets the `longitude` and `latitude` to zero. We need to make sure that the initializer of `Location` assigns the `coordinate` argument to its property in the test.

 You might have noticed that we have omitted the `message` parameter in the `XCTAssertEqual()` function. The reason is that the used assertion already gives enough context to figure out what we expect in the test. We expect that the two values are the same. There is no need to duplicate that information in the `message`. If you find that information useful, feel free to add `message` yourself.

The test does not compile because `CLLocationCoordinate2D` is an unresolved identifier. We need to import `CoreLocation` in `LocationTests.swift`:

```swift
import XCTest
@testable import ToDo
import CoreLocation
```

The test still does not compile because `Location` does not have a `coordinate` property yet. Similar to `ToDoItem`, we would like to have a short initializer for locations that only have a `name` argument. Therefore, we need to implement the initializer ourselves, and we cannot use the one provided by Swift. Replace the contents of `Location.swift` with the following lines of code:

```
import Foundation
import CoreLocation


struct Location {
    let name: String
    let coordinate: CLLocationCoordinate2D?

    init(name: String,
            coordinate: CLLocationCoordinate2D? = nil) {
        self.name = ""
        self.coordinate = coordinate
    }
}
```

Now run the tests. All the tests pass.

Note that we have intentionally set `name` in the initializer to an empty string. This is the easiest implementation that makes the tests pass. But it is clearly not what we want. The initializer should set the `name` of the `location` to the value in the `name` argument. So, we need another test to make sure that `name` is set correctly.

Add the following test to `LocationTests`:

```
func test_Init_SetsName() {
    let location = Location(name: "Foo")

    XCTAssertEqual(location.name, "Foo")
}
```

Run the test to make sure it fails. To make the test pass, change `self.name = ""` in the initializer of `Location` to `self.name = name`. Run the tests again to check whether they all pass now. There is nothing to refactor in the tests and implementation. Let's move on.

Implementing the ItemManager class

The to-do app will show all the to-do items in a list. The list of items will be managed by a class called `ItemManager`. It will expose an interface to get, add, and remove items.

Open Project Navigator and select the `ToDoTests` group. Go to the **iOS | Source | Unit Test Case** class to create a test case class with the name `ItemManagerTests`, and put it in the `Model` folder. Import the `ToDo` module (`@testable import ToDo`) and remove the two test method templates.

Count

The requirements of `Chapter 2`, *Planning and Structuring Your Test-Driven iOS App*, ask for a list with unchecked to-do items at the top and checked to-do items at the bottom of the list in the app. How the items are presented is not a matter of concern with regard to the model. But it has to be possible to get the number of unchecked and checked to-do items from the item manager.

Add the following code to `ItemManagerTests`:

```
func test_ToDoCount_Initially_IsZero() {
  let sut = ItemManager()
}
```

The `sut` abbreviation stands for **System Under Test**. We could also write this as `itemManager`, but using `sut` makes it easier to read, and it also allows us to copy and paste test code into other tests when appropriate.

The test is not yet finished, but it already fails because `ItemManager` is an unresolved identifier. Open Project Navigator again and select the `ToDo` group. Go to **iOS | Source | Swift File**. This will create a Swift file; let's call it `ItemManager.swift`, and select the `Model` folder as the file location.

Add the following class definition:

```
class ItemManager {
}
```

This is enough to make the test code compilable. Run the tests to make sure that all the tests pass and we can continue writing tests. In `test_ToDoCount_Initially_IsZero()`, add the assert function highlighted in the following code:

```
func test_ToDoCount_Initially_IsZero() {
    let sut = ItemManager()

    XCTAssertEqual(sut.toDoCount, 0)
}
```

With this addition, the test method tests whether `ItemManager` has the `toDoCount` property and whether it is initially set to zero.

The test still does not compile again because `Value of type 'ItemManager' has no member 'toDoCount'`. The simplest way to make the test pass is to add the following property declaration to `ItemManager`:

```
let toDoCount = 0
```

Run the tests. All the tests pass. The code and tests look good, so we do not need to refactor them.

In addition to the unchecked items, we also need to be able to get the number of checked items from the item manager. Add the following test to `ItemManagerTests`:

```
func test_DoneCount_Initially_IsZero() {
    let sut = ItemManager()

    XCTAssertEqual(sut.doneCount, 0)
}
```

To make this test pass, add the following property definition to `ItemManager`:

```
let doneCount = 0
```

Run the tests to check that this is enough to make them pass. If we look at the previously written test methods, we'll see a repetition. The `sut` variable is initialized in each test method. Let's refactor the test methods and remove the repetition. Add the following property declaration to the beginning of `ItemManagerTests`:

```
var sut: ItemManager!
```

Then, at the end of `setUp()`, add this initialization of `sut`:

```
sut = ItemManager()
```

Add the line `sut = nil` in `tearDown()` right before `super.tearDown()`. Now, we can remove the initialization from the tests:

```
func test_ToDoCount_Initially_IsZero() {
  XCTAssertEqual(sut.toDoCount, 0)
}


func test_DoneCount_Initially_IsZero() {
  XCTAssertEqual(sut.doneCount, 0)
}
```

Run the tests again to make sure that we have not broken anything with the refactoring.

Adding and checking items

The item manager should be able to add items to the list. Therefore, it should provide a method that takes an item. Later, we can call this method from the `ViewController` that will provide a UI to add items. Add the following code to `ItemManagerTests`:

```
func test_AddItem_IncreasesToDoCountToOne() {
  sut.add(ToDoItem(title: ""))
}
```

Here, we assume that `ItemManager` has an `add(_:)` method. You can see how TDD helps us think about the class/struct interface before a feature is implemented.

The `ItemManager` class does not have an `add(_:)` method and the test does not compile. Let's add the simplest implementation of `add(_:)`:

```
func add(_ item: ToDoItem) {
}
```

Run the tests to make sure they all pass. Now, we need to assert that after adding an item, `toDoCount` is 1. Add the following assert to `test_AddItem_IncreasesToDoCountToOne()`:

```
XCTAssertEqual(sut.toDoCount, 1)
```

Run the tests. The tests fail because `toDoCount` is a constant, and therefore, it never changes. Replace the highlighted lines in `ItemManager`:

```
class ItemManager {
    var toDoCount = 0
    let doneCount = 0

    func add(_ item: ToDoItem) {
        toDoCount += 1
    }
}
```

We have converted the `toDoCount` constant into a variable and added code in `add(_:)` to increase its value.

Run the tests. Everything works. The code and tests look good and there is nothing to refactor.

Nevertheless, the code clearly does not do what we intend it to. The item passed into `add(_:)` is not used or stored at all. This is a sign that we need another test.

The to-do items need to be presented to the user somehow. Therefore, `ItemManager` needs to provide a method that returns an item. Add the following code to `ItemManagerTests`:

```
func test_ItemAt_ReturnsAddedItem() {
    let item = ToDoItem(title: "Foo")
    sut.add(item)

    let returnedItem = sut.item(at: 0)
}
```

At this point, we have to stop writing the test because this code does not compile. There is no `item(at:)` method in `ItemManager` yet. We need to add it before we can continue with the test. Add the following to `ItemManager`:

```
func item(at index: Int) -> ToDoItem {
    return ToDoItem(title: "")
}
```

It is the simplest implementation that makes the test code compilable again. Now, add the following assert to `test_ItemAt_ReturnsAddedItem()`:

```
XCTAssertEqual(returnedItem.title, item.title)
```

The test fails because `item(at:)` returns an item with an empty title. To fix it, we need to add an array to store the item passed into `add(_:)`, and use the same array to return the item again in `item(at:)`. Replace the implementation of `ItemManager` with the following code:

```
class ItemManager {
    var toDoCount = 0
    let doneCount = 0
    private var toDoItems: [ToDoItem] = []

    func add(_ item: ToDoItem) {
        toDoCount += 1
        toDoItems.append(item)
    }

    func item(at index: Int) -> ToDoItem {
        return toDoItems[index]
    }
}
```

Let's go through the changes step by step. We have added a `toDoItems` array to store the to-do items. The array is private because we want to encapsulate the underlying array. In `add(_:)`, the item that's passed in is added to the array. And in `item(at:)`, the item at the specified index is returned.

Run the tests. All the tests pass and there is nothing to refactor.

The user has to be able to check the items. The checked items need to be accessible from the item manager. Add the following code to `ItemManagerTests`:

```
func test_CheckItemAt_ChangesCounts() {
    sut.add(ToDoItem(title: ""))

    sut.checkItem(at: 0)
}
```

This code does not compile because there is no `checkItem(at:)` method in `ItemManager`. To make the test code compilable, add it to `ItemManager`:

```
func checkItem(at index: Int) {
}
```

When the user checks an item, `toDoCount` should decrease and `doneCount` should increase. Add the following asserts to `test_CheckAt_ChangesCounts()`:

```
XCTAssertEqual(sut.toDoCount, 0)
XCTAssertEqual(sut.doneCount, 1)
```

To make this test pass, we simply decrease and increase the values. A possible implementation looks like this:

```
class ItemManager {
    var toDoCount = 0
    var doneCount = 0
    private var toDoItems: [ToDoItem] = []

    // ... other methods ...

    func checkItem(at index: Int) {
        toDoCount -= 1
        doneCount += 1
    }
}
```

This is the simplest implementation that makes the tests pass. Again, the code clearly does not do what we have planned. When checking an item, it should be removed from the `toDoItems` array. We need another test to ensure that it implements this behavior:

```
func test_CheckItemAt_RemovesItFromToDoItems() {
    let first = ToDoItem(title: "First")
    let second = ToDoItem(title: "Second")
    sut.add(first)
    sut.add(second)

    sut.checkItem(at: 0)

    XCTAssertEqual(sut.item(at: 0).title,
                   "Second")
}
```

This test fails. To make it pass, add the following line to `checkItemAtIndex(_:)`:

```
_ = toDoItems.remove(at: index)
```

This code uses the `remove(at:)` method of the built-in array type. Run the tests. All the tests pass. There is nothing further to refactor.

In the app, the checked items will be shown below the unchecked items. This means that `ItemManager` also needs to provide a method that returns checked items. Add the following code to `ItemManagerTests`:

```swift
func test_DoneItemAt_ReturnsCheckedItem() {
  let item = ToDoItem(title: "Foo")
  sut.add(item)

  sut.checkItem(at: 0)
  let returnedItem = sut.doneItem(at: 0)
}
```

Before we can continue writing the test, we need to add `doneItem(at:)` to `ItemManager`:

```swift
func doneItem(at index: Int) -> ToDoItem {
  return ToDoItem(title: "")
}
```

Again, this is the simplest implementation to make the test pass, so let's continue writing the test. Add the following assert to `test_DoneItemAt_ReturnsCheckedItem()`:

```swift
XCTAssertEqual(returnedItem.title, item.title)
```

This test fails because we return a dummy item from `doneItem(at:)`. To make it pass, replace the implementation of `ItemManager` with the following code:

```swift
class ItemManager {
  var toDoCount = 0
  var doneCount = 0
  private var toDoItems: [ToDoItem] = []
  private var doneItems: [ToDoItem] = []

  func add(_ item: ToDoItem) {
    toDoCount += 1
    toDoItems.append(item)
  }

  func item(at index: Int) -> ToDoItem {
    return toDoItems[index]
  }

  func checkItem(at index: Int) {
    toDoCount -= 1
    doneCount += 1

    let item = toDoItems.remove(at: index)
    doneItems.append(item)
  }
```

```
func doneItem(at index: Int) -> ToDoItem {
    return doneItems[index]
}
}
```

We have added a doneItems array to store the checked items. In checkItem(at:), we take the item removed from toDoItems and add it to doneItems. In doneItem(at:), we simply return the item for the passed in index from the doneItems array.

Run the tests. All the tests pass. But there is a small thing we should refactor. The todoCount and doneCount variables are always the same as the count of the toDoItems and doneItems arrays, respectively. So, replace the todoCount and doneCount variables with computed properties:

```
var toDoCount: Int { return toDoItems.count }
var doneCount: Int { return doneItems.count }
```

Remove the lines with the toDoCount += 1, todoCount -= 1, and doneCount += 1 statements. Run the tests to make sure that everything still works.

There is something else that should be improved. To assert the equality of ToDoItem instances, we have used assert functions like this:

```
XCTAssertEqual(returnedItem.title, item.title)
```

We would, however, like to write them like this:

```
XCTAssertEqual(returnedItem, item)
```

If we try to do this and run the tests, we get this error:

```
error: cannot invoke 'XCTAssertEqual' with an argument list of type
'(ToDoItem, ToDoItem)'
```

To figure out what this means, let's have a look at the definition of XCTAssertEqual:

```
public func XCTAssertEqual<T : Equatable>(_ expression1: @autoclosure ()
throws -> T, _ expression2: @autoclosure () throws -> T, _ message:
@autoclosure () -> String = default, file: StaticString = #file, line: UInt
= #line)
```

The important information here is <T : Equatable>. It indicates that we can only use XCTAsserEqual to check whether two elements are equal when they have the same type, and this type should conform to the Equatable protocol. We could stop here and decide that we do not need to make ToDoItem conform to Equatable, just to make the tests clearer. We can always compare each property of the items. But test code is still code. It should be easy to read and to understand.

In addition to this, we would like to make sure that the user cannot add the same item to the list twice because doing this does not add any value to the app. In fact, it could be considered a bug. To check whether an item is already managed by the list, we need to also be able to easily check whether two items represent the same information. This again means that to-do items need to be Equatable. In the next few sections, we will add conformance to Equatable, ToDoItem, and Location.

Before we continue, replace the assertion in the last test with the assertion we had earlier:

```
XCTAssertEqual(returnedItem.title, item.title)
```

Run the tests again to make sure that we start from a green state.

Equatable

 At the time of writing, conformance to the protocol Equatable had to be implemented by the developer. But at the same time, there is a discussion about whether the compiler will be able to generate the necessary code in the future. So, maybe by the time you read this section, it's enough to add Equatable in the definition of a class or struct to make it conform to Equatable. In this case, you can skip this section.

Open ToDoItemTests.swift in the editor and ToDoItem.swift in the Assistant Editor. We would like to be able to compare to-do items using XCTAssertEqual. Add the following test to ToDoItemTests to drive the implementation of the Equatable conformance:

```
func text_EqualItems_AreEqual() {
  let first = ToDoItem(title: "Foo")
  let second = ToDoItem(title: "Foo")

  XCTAssertEqual(first, second)
}
```

The static analyzer tells us that it `Cannot invoke 'XCTAssertEqual' with an argument list of type '(ToDoItem, ToDoItem)'`. This is because `ToDoItem` is not `Equatable`. Make `ToDoItem` conform to `Equatable` like this:

```
struct ToDoItem : Equatable {
  // ...
}
```

Now, we get an error saying that `'ToDoItem' does not conform to the 'Equatable' protocol`. The `Equatable` protocol looks like this for Swift 3.0:

```
public protocol Equatable {
    public static func ==(lhs: Self, rhs: Self) -> Bool
}
```

So, we need to implement the `==` equivalence operator for `ToDoItem`. The operator needs to be defined in a global scope. At the end of `ToDoItem.swift` outside of the `ToDoItem` class, add the following code:

```
func ==(lhs: ToDoItem, rhs: ToDoItem) -> Bool {
  return true
}
```

Run the tests. The tests pass and, again, there is nothing to refactor.

The implementation of the equivalence operator is strange because it doesn't check any properties of the items that are passed in. But following the rules of TDD, it is good enough. Let's move on to more complicated tests:

```
func test_Items_WhenLocationDiffers_AreNotEqual() {
  let first = ToDoItem(title: "",
                       location: Location(name: "Foo"))
  let second = ToDoItem(title: "",
                        location: Location(name: "Bar"))

  XCTAssertNotEqual(first, second)
}
```

The two items differ in terms of their location names. Run the test. It fails because the equivalence operator always returns `true`. But it should return `false` if the locations differ. Replace the implementation of the operator with this code:

```
func ==(lhs: ToDoItem, rhs: ToDoItem) -> Bool {
    if lhs.location != rhs.location {
      return false
    }
    return true
}
```

Again, the static analyzer complains. This is because this time, `Location` does not conform to `Equatable`. In fact, `Location` needs to be `Equatable` too. But before we can move to `Location` and its tests, we need to have all tests pass again. Replace the highlighted line in the equivalence operator to make all the tests pass again:

```
func ==(lhs: ToDoItem, rhs: ToDoItem) -> Bool {
    if lhs.location?.name != rhs.location?.name {
      return false
    }
    return true
}
```

For now, we just test whether the names of the locations differ. Later, when `Location` conforms to `Equatable`, we will be able to compare locations directly.

Open `LocationTests.swift` in the editor and `Location.swift` in the Assistant Editor. Add the following test to `LocationTests`:

```
func test_EqualLocations_AreEqual() {
    let first = Location(name: "Foo")
    let second = Location(name: "Foo")
    XCTAssertEqual(first, second)
}
```

Again, this code does not compile because `Location` does not conform to `Equatable`. Let's add the `Equatable` conformance. Replace the `struct` declaration with this:

```
struct Location : Equatable {
    // ...
}
```

Add the dummy implementation of the equivalence operator in `Location.swift`, but outside of the `Location` struct:

```
public static func ==(lhs: Location,
                      rhs: Location) -> Bool {

    return true
}
```

Run the tests. All the tests pass again, and at this point, there is nothing to refactor. Add the following test:

```
func test_Locations_WhenLatitudeDiffers_AreNotEqual() {
    let firstCoordinate =
      CLLocationCoordinate2D(latitude: 1.0,
                             longitude: 0.0)
    let first = Location(name: "Foo",
                    coordinate: firstCoordinate)

    let secondCoordinate =
      CLLocationCoordinate2D(latitude: 0.0,
                             longitude: 0.0)
    let second = Location(name: "Foo",
                    coordinate: secondCoordinate)

    XCTAssertNotEqual(first, second)
}
```

The two locations differ in terms of latitude. Run the test. This test fails because the equivalence operator always returns `true`. Replace the implementation of the equivalence operator with the following code:

```
public static func ==(lhs: Location,
                      rhs: Location) -> Bool {

    if lhs.coordinate?.latitude !=
       rhs.coordinate?.latitude {

        return false
    }

    return true
}
```

In case the `latitude` of the location's coordinates differ, the operator returns `false`; otherwise, it returns `true`. Run the tests. All the tests pass again. Next, we need to make sure that the locations that differ in terms of `longitude` are not equal. Add the following test:

```
func test_Locations_WhenLongitudeDiffers_AreNotEqual() {
    let firstCoordinate =
      CLLocationCoordinate2D(latitude: 0.0,
                             longitude: 1.0)
    let first = Location(name: "Foo",
                    coordinate: firstCoordinate)

    let secondCoordinate =
      CLLocationCoordinate2D(latitude: 0.0,
                             longitude: 0.0)
    let second = Location(name: "Foo",
                    coordinate: secondCoordinate)

    XCTAssertNotEqual(first, second)
}
```

Run the test. This test fails because we do not check `longitude` in the equivalence operator yet. Add the highlighted lines to the operator:

```
public static func ==(lhs: Location,
                      rhs: Location) -> Bool {

    if lhs.coordinate?.latitude !=
      rhs.coordinate?.latitude {

      return false
    }
    if lhs.coordinate?.longitude !=
      rhs.coordinate?.longitude {

      return false
    }

    return true
}
```

Run the tests. All the tests pass again. The last two tests that we have written are very similar to each other. The only difference is the definition of the first coordinate. Let's refactor the test code to make it clearer to read and easier to maintain. First, we create a method that performs the tests that are given different values for the Location properties:

```
func assertLocationNotEqualWith(firstName: String,
                                firstLongLat: (Double, Double)?,
                                secondName: String,
                                secondLongLat: (Double, Double)?) {
  var firstCoord: CLLocationCoordinate2D? = nil
  if let firstLongLat = firstLongLat {
    firstCoord =
      CLLocationCoordinate2D(latitude: firstLongLat.0,
                             longitude: firstLongLat.1)
  }
  let firstLocation =
    Location(name: firstName,
             coordinate: firstCoord)
  var secondCoord: CLLocationCoordinate2D? = nil
  if let secondLongLat = secondLongLat {
    secondCoord =
      CLLocationCoordinate2D(latitude: secondLongLat.0,
                             longitude: secondLongLat.1)
  }
  let secondLocation =
    Location(name: secondName,
             coordinate: secondCoord)
  XCTAssertNotEqual(firstLocation, secondLocation)
}
```

This method takes two strings and optional tuples, respectively. With this information, it creates two Location instances and compares them using XCTAssertNotEqual.

Now, we can replace test_Locations_WhenLatitudeDiffers_AreNotEqual() with this:

```
func test_Locations_WhenLatitudeDiffers_AreNotEqual() {
  assertLocationNotEqualWith(firstName: "Foo",
                             firstLongLat: (1.0, 0.0),
                             secondName: "Foo",
                             secondLongLat: (0.0, 0.0))
}
```

To check whether this test still works, we need to make it fail by removing some implementation code. If the test passes again when we re-add the code, we can be confident that the test still works. In `Location.swift`, remove the check for the nonequality of latitude:

```
if lhs.coordinate?.latitude != rhs.coordinate?.latitude {
    return false
}
```

Run the test. The test does indeed fail, but the failure shows in the line where `XCTAssertNotEqual` is located:

```
82    func assertLocationNotEqualWith(firstName: String,
83                                    firstLongLat: (Double,
84                                                   Double)?,
85                          secondName: String,
86                          secondLongLat: (Double,
87                                          Double)?) {
88
89        var firstCoord: CLLocationCoordinate2D? = nil
90        if let firstLongLat = firstLongLat {
91          firstCoord =
92            CLLocationCoordinate2D(latitude: firstLongLat.0,
93                                   longitude: firstLongLat.1)
94        }
95        let firstLocation =
96          Location(name: firstName,
97                   coordinate: firstCoord)
98
99
100       var secondCoord: CLLocationCoordinate2D? = nil
101       if let secondLongLat = secondLongLat {
102         secondCoord =
103           CLLocationCoordinate2D(latitude: secondLongLat.0,
104                                  longitude: secondLongLat.1)
105       }
106       let secondLocation =
107         Location(name: secondName,
108                  coordinate: secondCoord)
109
110
111       XCTAssertNotEqual(firstLocation, secondLocation)  ◆ XCTAssertNotEqual faile...
112   }
```

We would like to see the failure in the test method. In Chapter 1, *Your First Unit Tests*, we discussed how to change the line for which the failure is reported. The easiest way to do this is to add the `line` argument to `assertLocationNotEqualWith(...)` and use it in the assertion:

```
func assertLocationNotEqualWith(firstName: String,
                                firstLongLat: (Double, Double)?,
                                secondName: String,
                                secondLongLat: (Double, Double)?,
                                line: UInt) {

    // ...

    XCTAssertNotEqual(firstLocation,
                      secondLocation,
                      line: line)
}
```

In `test_Locations_WhenLatitudeDiffers_AreNotEqual()`, we need to call this method like this:

```
assertLocationNotEqualWith(firstName: "Foo",
                           firstLongLat: (1.0, 0.0),
                           secondName: "Foo",
                           secondLongLat: (0.0, 0.0),
                           line: 64)
```

The number 64 is the line number at which the method call starts in my case. This could be different for you. Run the tests again. The failure is now reported on the specified line.

We cannot be satisfied with this solution. A hardcoded value for the line number is a bad idea. What if we want to add a test at the beginning of the class or add something to `setUp()`? Then, we would have to change the `line` argument of all the calls of that function. There has to be a better way of doing this.

C has some magic macros that are also available when writing Swift code. Replace 64 (or whatever you have put there) with the `#line` magic macro. Run the tests again. Now, the failure is reported in the line where the magic macro is. This is good enough even if the method call is spread over several lines.

We can do better using default values for method arguments. Add a default value to the last argument of `assertLocationNotEqualWith(...)`:

```
line: UInt = #line
```

As the method now has a default value for the last argument, we can remove it from the call:

```
assertLocationNotEqualWith(firstName: "Foo",
                    firstLongLat: (1.0, 0.0),
                    secondName: "Foo",
                    secondLongLat: (0.0, 0.0))
```

Run the tests again. The failure is now reported at the beginning of the call, but without the need to hardcode the line number. Add the code again to the equivalence operator that we had to remove in order to make the test fail:

```
if lhs.coordinate?.latitude != rhs.coordinate?.latitude {
    return false
}
```

Run the tests to make sure that all of them pass again. Now, replace `test_Locations_WhenLongitudeDiffers_AreNotEqual()` with the following code:

```
func test_Locations_WhenLongitudeDiffers_AreNotEqual() {

assertLocationNotEqualWith(firstName: "Foo",
                    firstLongLat: (0.0, 1.0),
                    secondName: "Foo",
                    secondLongLat: (0.0, 0.0))
}
```

Run the tests. All the tests pass.

If one location has a coordinate set and the other one does not, they should be considered to be different. Add the following test to make sure that the equivalence operator works this way:

```
func test_Locations_WhenOnlyOneHasCoordinate_AreNotEqual() {

assertLocationNotEqualWith(firstName: "Foo",
                    firstLongLat: (0.0, 0.0),
                    secondName: "Foo",
                    secondLongLat: nil)
}
```

Run the tests. All the tests pass. The current implementation of the equivalence operator already works in this way.

Right now, two locations with the same coordinate but different names are equivalent. But we want them to be considered different. Add the following test:

```
func test_Locations_WhenNamesDiffer_AreNotEqual() {
    assertLocationNotEqualWith(firstName: "Foo",
                               firstLongLat: nil,
                               secondName: "Bar",
                               secondLongLat: nil)
}
```

This test fails. Add the following `if` condition right before the `return true` line in the implementation of the equivalence operator:

```
if lhs.name != rhs.name {
    return false
}
```

Run the tests again. All the tests pass and there is nothing to refactor.

The `Location` struct now conforms to `Equatable`. Let's go back to `ToDoItem` and continue where we left off.

First, let's refactor the current implementation of the equivalence operator of `ToDoItem`. Now that `Location` conforms to `Equatable`, we can check whether the two locations are different using the `!=` operator (which we get for free by implementing the `==` operator):

```
public static func ==(lhs: ToDoItem,
                      rhs: ToDoItem) -> Bool {
    if lhs.location != rhs.location {
        return false
    }
    return true
}
```

Run the tests. All the tests pass and there is nothing to refactor.

If one to-do item has a location and the other does not, they are not equal. Add the following test to `ToDoItemTests` to make sure this is the case:

```
func test_Items_WhenOneLocationIsNil_AreNotEqual() {
    let first = ToDoItem(title: "",
                         location: Location(name: "Foo"))
    let second = ToDoItem(title: "",
                          location: nil)
    XCTAssertNotEqual(first, second)
}
```

The test already passes. Let's make sure that it also works the other way round. Change the `let` keywords to `var`, and add the following code to the end of `test_Items_WhenOneLocationIsNil_AreNotEqual()`:

```
first = ToDoItem(title: "",
                      location: nil)
second = ToDoItem(title: "",
                      location: Location(name: "Foo"))

XCTAssertNotEqual(first, second)
```

Run the tests. This also works with the current implementation of the equivalence operator of `ToDoItem`.

Next, if the `timestamp` of two to-do items differs, they are different. The following code tests whether this is the case in our implementation:

```
func test_Items_WhenTimestampsDiffer_AreNotEqual() {


    let first = ToDoItem(title: "Foo",
                          timestamp: 1.0)
    let second = ToDoItem(title: "Foo",
                          timestamp: 0.0)

    XCTAssertNotEqual(first, second)
}
```

Both to-do items are equivalent to each other, except for the `timestamp`. The test fails because we do not compare the `timestamp` in the equivalence operator yet. Add the following `if` condition in the operator implementation right before the `return true` statement:

```
if lhs.timestamp != rhs.timestamp {
  return false
}
```

Run the tests. All the tests pass and there is nothing to refactor. From the tests about the equivalence of the `Location` instances, we already know that this implementation is enough even if one of the timestamps is `nil`. So, no more tests for the equivalence of timestamps are needed.

Now, let's make sure that two to-do items that differ in their descriptions are not equal. Add this test:

```
func test_Items_WhenDescriptionsDiffer_AreNotEqual() {

    let first = ToDoItem(title: "Foo",
                         itemDescription: "Bar")
    let second = ToDoItem(title: "Foo",
                          itemDescription: "Baz")

    XCTAssertNotEqual(first, second)
}
```

Adding the following `if` condition to the equivalence operator right before the `return true` statement, makes the test pass:

```
if lhs.itemDescription != rhs.itemDescription {
    return false
}
```

The last thing we have to check is whether two to-do items differ if their titles differ. Add this test:

```
func test_Items_WhenTitlesDiffer_AreNotEqual() {
    let first = ToDoItem(title: "Foo")
    let second = ToDoItem(title: "Bar")

    XCTAssertNotEqual(first, second)
}
```

With all the experience we have gained in this section, the implementation nearly writes itself. Add another `if` condition again right before the `return true` statement:

```
if lhs.title != rhs.title {
    return false
}
```

Run the tests. All the tests pass.

Now that `ToDoItem` and `Location` conform to `Equatable`, the to-do items and locations can be used directly in `XCTAssertEqual`. Go through the tests and make the necessary changes.

Removing all items

The `ItemManager` class needs to provide a method to remove all items. Add the following code to `ItemManagerTests`:

```
func test_RemoveAll_ResultsInCountsBeZero() {

    sut.add(ToDoItem(title: "Foo"))
    sut.add(ToDoItem(title: "Bar"))
    sut.checkItem(at: 0)

    XCTAssertEqual(sut.toDoCount, 1)
    XCTAssertEqual(sut.doneCount, 1)

    sut.removeAll()
}
```

This code adds two to-do items to the manager and checks one item. Then, it asserts that the count of the items has the expected values and calls `removeAll()`.

The code does not compile because `removeAll()` is not implemented yet. Add the minimal implementation needed to make the test code compilable:

```
func removeAll() {
}
```

Now, add the following assertions to `test_RemoveAll_ResultsInCountsBeZero()` to check whether the items have been removed:

```
XCTAssertEqual(sut.toDoCount, 0)
XCTAssertEqual(sut.doneCount, 0)
```

To make this test pass, we need to remove all the items from the underlying arrays. Add the following implementation in `removeAll()`:

```
toDoItems.removeAll()
doneItems.removeAll()
```

Run the tests. All the tests pass and there is nothing to refactor.

Ensuring uniqueness

As mentioned earlier, we would like to make sure that each to-do item can only be added to the list once. To ensure this behavior is implemented, add the following test to `ItemManagerTests`:

```
func test_Add_WhenItemIsAlreadyAdded_DoesNotIncreaseCount() {

    sut.add(ToDoItem(title: "Foo"))
    sut.add(ToDoItem(title: "Foo"))

    XCTAssertEqual(sut.toDoCount, 1)
}
```

This test fails. To make the test pass, we need to check whether the item we want to add to the list is already contained in the list. Fortunately, Swift provides a method on the array type that does exactly this. Replace `add(_:)` with the following code:

```
func add(_ item: ToDoItem) {

    if !toDoItems.contains(item) {

        toDoItems.append(item)
    }
}
```

Run the tests. All the tests pass, and we are finally finished with the implementation of our model.

Summary

In this chapter, we took a look at how to implement the model layer of our app using TDD. We followed the TDD workflow (red, green, and refactor) to guide the implementation of the required micro features.

We implemented two model structs and a manager class. We added conformance to the `Equatable` protocol for the model structs in order to make sure that the same to-do item cannot be added to the list more than once. We also encapsulated the internals of the manager class with methods to add, receive, and remove to-do items from the manager.

TDD led us to a clean, simple, and fully-tested model.

In the next chapter, we will implement the controller layer and the view layer following the Model-View-Controller design pattern using TDD.

4
A Test-Driven View Controller

View controllers are glue-like components that hold an app together. They are responsible for the moderation between the model and the view layer. As moderators, they are highly-specialized according to the needs of the model and the user interface they belong to. As a result, the controller layer is often not reusable in other parts of the app, or even in other apps.

As the controller is responsible for many different tasks, it often becomes large. It is a good practice, therefore, to construct the controller layer of a specific feature out of different controller classes. For instance, beginners often put their networking code into the same class that is responsible for filling the UI with information. This results in a so-called god class, a class that knows and controls everything.

Such classes are hard to write, read, and maintain, and should, therefore, be avoided. To make the view controller that's showing the list of items clean, we need to separate the data source and delegate the table view out into its own class, the data provider. The communication between the view controller and the data provider can be defined using protocols. This way, you can swap one implementation for another by just conforming to the protocol. In addition to this, when defining a protocol, you need to think about how to make the API surface (that is, the number of methods that are exposed to other classes) small and easy to understand. The result of this will be a modular architecture with a clear separation of tasks into different classes and structs.

In this chapter, we will build the different classes that make up the controller layer of our app. In a later chapter, we will put all the modules we have implemented together in a running app.

We'll cover the following topics in this chapter:

- Implementing `ItemListViewController`
- Implementing `DataProvider`

- Implementing `DetailViewController`
- Implementing `InputViewController`

Implementing ItemListViewController

Let's start with the list showing the to-do items. This is the most important view controller. It is the first view that a user sees when the app has started.

This controller is also responsible for presenting the input screen that allows the user to add to-do items to the list. In addition, it also presents the detail screen that shows the details of selected to-do items.

We first need to structure the files in the Project Navigator in order to enable seamless navigation between the different files. Select the three model files that we already have (`ToDoItem.swift`, `Location.swift`, and `ItemManager.swift`), and hold down the *ctrl* key while you click on one of the selected files. Xcode presents a menu similar to what's shown in the following screenshot:

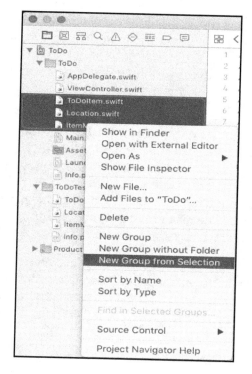

Select **New Group from Selection** and call it `Model`. Do the same in the test target with the corresponding test cases.

With an easy-to-navigate project in the Project Navigator, let's return to the TDD workflow. To drive the implementation of `ItemListViewController`, we need a test case to collect the tests.

Select the `ToDoTests` group and add **Unit Test Case Class**. Put in the name `ItemListViewControllerTest` and click on **Next**. Click on **Create**. As demonstrated in the previous chapters, add the import statement `@testable import ToDo` and remove the two template test methods.

The data will be presented to the user using a table view. We need a test to make sure that `ItemListViewController` has a table view and that it is set after `viewDidLoad()`. Add the following code to `ItemListViewControllerTests`:

```
func test_TableViewIsNotNilAfterViewDidLoad() {
    let sut = ItemListViewController()
}
```

The static analyzer complains that `ItemListViewController` is an unresolved identifier. We have seen this message so often that we already expected this to happen. There is no `ItemListViewController` yet. Select the `ToDo` group in the Project Navigator in Xcode, and go to **File | New | File...** Create **iOS | Source | Cocoa Touch Class**, name it `ItemListViewController`, make it a subclass of `UIViewController`, and click on **Next**. Click on **Create**. Remove the code within the `ItemListViewController` class so that it looks like the following snippet:

```
import UIKit

class ItemListViewController: UIViewController {
}
```

To make writing tests easier, set up the Xcode window as you did earlier, with the test case on the left-hand side and the implementation code in the Assistant Editor on the right-hand side. Run the tests to make sure that we have set up everything correctly.

Add the following code at the end of `test_TableView_AfterViewDidLoad_IsNotNil()`:

```
sut.loadViewIfNeeded()

XCTAssertNotNil(sut.tableView)
```

The line `sut.loadViewIfNeeded()` triggers the call of `viewDidLoad()`. Never call `viewDidLoad()` directly.

Again, the static analyzer complains. This is because of `Value of type 'ItemListViewController' has no member 'tableView'`. To fix this, add the `tableView` property:

```
var tableView: UITableView?
```

Run the test. It should compile but fail. This is because we are not testing whether the property is present, but if the property is set to a value different from `nil` after `viewDidLoad()` has been called, and we have not done anything in the implementation to set it to some value.

This is the simplest implementation to make the test pass:

```
override func viewDidLoad() {
    super.viewDidLoad()

    tableView = UITableView()
}
```

Run the tests to make sure that all the tests pass.

After following the rules of TDD, we've done enough for now and the code looks clean, so there should be nothing to refactor. At this point, however, we need to make a decision. Do we want to implement the UI using **Interface Builder** (**IB**) in Xcode, or do we want to implement it completely in code?

IB has improved a lot over the last few years, and using storyboards can speed up the development of a small app, especially when you are not experienced in building user interfaces in code. In addition to this, you get a preview of what the UI will look like while you are building it. For larger projects, I would recommend that you at least have a look at how UIs are built without IB, because it is often easier to reason and maintain that way.

We will use IB for our project because TDD does not help a lot with UIs, and using IB gives us a clear-cut idea of what to test and what not to, as you would normally test the position and color of your UI elements.

When we created the project for our app, Xcode added a storyboard file, `Main.storyboard`, for the UI. Open Project Navigator and click on `Main.storyboard` to open it in IB. You will see something like the following screenshot:

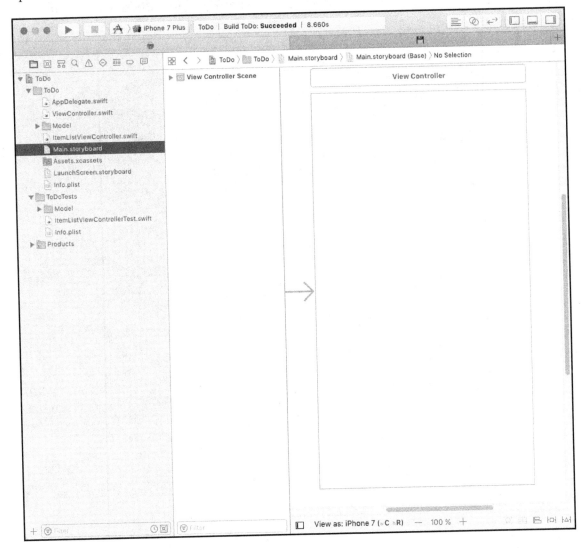

There is already a scene for a view controller in the storyboard, and there is also a `ViewController.swift` file from the Xcode template of a Single View Application. We won't use it, so let's remove the file and scene. First, select `ViewController.swift` and press the *Delete* key. Then, select the **View Controller** scene in the storyboard and press the *Delete* key again.

Now we have a clean slate to build the UI. Open the object library by going to **View** | **Utilities** | **Show Object Library**, and drag **View Controller** onto the storyboard. Change the class in Identity Inspector to `ItemListViewController`. Add a table view to the **View Controller**, make it fill up the scene, and add layout constraints to the edges of the super view as follows:

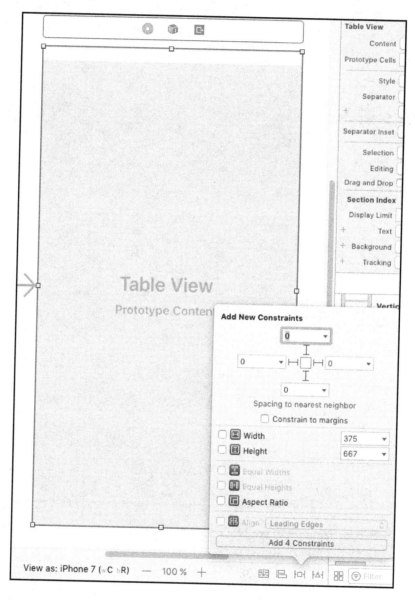

Open `ItemListViewController.swift` in the Assistant Editor and replace the `tableView` property with the following snippet:

```
@IBOutlet var tableView: UITableView!
```

Now, hold the *ctrl* key and drag from the table view in the storyboard scene to the `tableView` property to connect the two. Remove the implementation of `viewDidLoad()` and run the tests. The `test_TableView_AfterViewDidLoad_IsNotNil()` test fails because the `tableView` property is `nil` after `viewDidLoad()` is called. The reason for this is that we are not using the storyboard to instantiate the **View Controller** yet. By calling the `ItemListViewController()` initializer, we use the simple `init()` initializer. But we need to use the storyboard to create the **Item List View Controller**.

Open the storyboard and set **Storyboard ID** to `ItemListViewController` in Identity Inspector. Replace `test_TableView_AfterViewDidLoad_IsNotNil()` with the following code:

```
func test_TableView_AfterViewDidLoad_IsNotNil() {
    let storyboard = UIStoryboard(name: "Main",
                                  bundle: nil)
    let viewController =
      storyboard.instantiateViewController(
        withIdentifier: "ItemListViewController")
    let sut = viewController
      as! ItemListViewController
    sut.loadViewIfNeeded()
    XCTAssertNotNil(sut.tableView)
}
```

This code first gets a reference to the `Main` storyboard, and then it instantiates an instance of `ItemListViewController` from the storyboard. This works because we have set the **Storyboard ID**.

Run the tests. Now, all the tests pass.

As mentioned previously, we would like to put the data source and delegate of the table view into a separate class. Add the following test to `ItemListViewControllerTests` to drive the implementation:

```
func test_LoadingView_SetsTableViewDataSource() {
    let storyboard = UIStoryboard(name: "Main",
                                      bundle: nil)
    let viewController =
      storyboard.instantiateViewController(
        withIdentifier: "ItemListViewController")
    let sut = viewController
      as! ItemListViewController

    sut.loadViewIfNeeded()

    XCTAssertTrue(sut.tableView.dataSource is ItemListDataProvider)
}
```

The assertion makes sure that the data source of the table view is of type `ItemListDataProvider`. To make the test compilable, we first need to add the `ItemListDataProvider` class. Select the **ToDo** group in the Project Navigator, and add an **iOS | Source | Cocoa Touch Class** called `ItemListDataProvider` as a subclass of `NSObject`.

Now the test compiles, but it fails because we need to set an instance of `ItemListDataProvider` as the data source of the table view. Let's add a property for the data provider to `ItemListViewController` as follows:

```
@IBOutlet var dataProvider: ItemListDataProvider!
```

We will connect the data provider with an element in the storyboard. Doing this has the advantage of the data provider being instantiated when the **View Controller** is loaded from the storyboard.

Open `Main.storyboard` and drag an object from the `object` library into the scene in the **Document Outline** of the storyboard, as shown in the following screenshot:

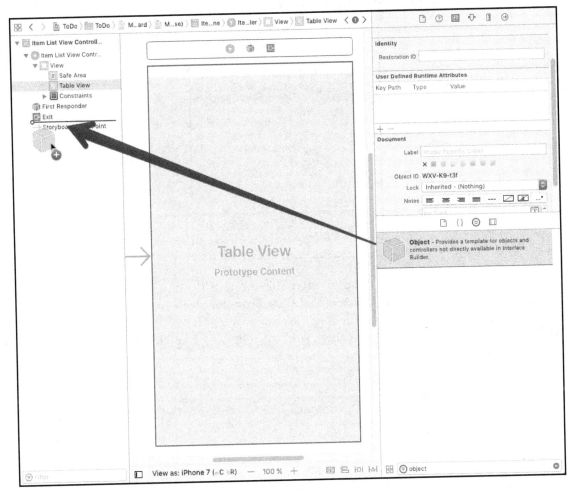

In the Identity Inspector, set the class to `ItemListDataProvider`. Hold down the *ctrl* key, and drag the **Document Outline** from the **Item List View Controller** to the **Item List Data Provider**, as shown in the following screenshot:

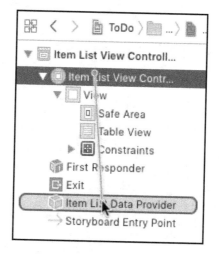

In the appearing pop-up, select **dataProvider**. This connects the `dataProvider` property in `ItemListViewController` to the **Item List Data Provider** object in the storyboard. Remember that we need to make sure that the data provider is set as the data source of the table view after `viewDidLoad()` is called. Add the following implementation of `viewDidLoad()` to `ItemListViewController`:

```
override func viewDidLoad() {
  super.viewDidLoad()

  tableView.dataSource = dataProvider
}
```

The static analyzer complains that `ItemListDataProvider` does not conform to the `UITableViewDataSource` protocol. To fix this, open `ItemListDataProvider` and replace the class implementation with the following code:

```
class ItemListDataProvider: NSObject, UITableViewDataSource {

  func tableView(_ tableView: UITableView,
                 numberOfRowsInSection section: Int) -> Int {

    return 0
  }
```

```
func tableView(_ tableView: UITableView,
               cellForRowAt indexPath: IndexPath) -> UITableViewCell {


    return UITableViewCell()
  }
}
```

Run the tests. All the tests pass, so let's take a look at whether there is something to refactor. In `ItemListViewController`, `dataProvider` is of the type `ItemListDataSource`. This is needed to make the connection between IB and the property. Now that we have the connection, we can replace the type with the `UITableViewDataSource` protocol:

```
@IBOutlet var dataProvider: UITableViewDataSource!
```

With this change, `ItemListViewController` only knows that `dataProvider` conforms to the `UITableViewDataSource` protocol. This means that the two classes are decoupled from each other, and there is a defined interface in the form of the protocol.

Run the tests to make sure that everything still works.

There is more to refactor. We have some code duplication in the test methods. Remove the following code from the test methods:

```
let storyboard = UIStoryboard(name: "Main",
                              bundle: nil)
let viewController =
  storyboard.instantiateViewController(
    withIdentifier: "ItemListViewController")
let sut = viewController as! ItemListViewController
sut.loadViewIfNeeded()
```

Add the `var sut: ItemListViewController!` property to `ItemListViewControllerTests`, and add the following code to `setUp()`:

```
let storyboard = UIStoryboard(name: "Main",
                              bundle: nil)
let viewController =
  storyboard.instantiateViewController(
    withIdentifier: "ItemListViewController")
sut = viewController as! ItemListViewController
sut.loadViewIfNeeded()
```

Run the tests again. Everything should still work.

Next, we need to make sure that the data provider is also the delegate of the table view. Add the following test to `ItemListViewControllerTests`:

```
func test_LoadingView_SetsTableViewDelegate() {
  XCTAssertTrue(sut.tableView.delegate is ItemListDataProvider)
}
```

To make the test pass, add the `UITableViewDelegate` conformance in the declaration of the `dataProvider` property, such that it looks like this:

```
@IBOutlet var dataProvider: (UITableViewDataSource & UITableiewDelegate)!
```

Add the following line at the end of `viewDidLoad()`:

```
tableView.delegate = dataProvider
```

Run the tests. All the tests pass.

The data source and delegate need to be the same instance because otherwise selecting a cell could result in showing the details of a completely different item. Add the following test:

```
func test_LoadingView_DataSourceEqualDelegate() {
  XCTAssertEqual(sut.tableView.dataSource as? ItemListDataProvider,
                 sut.tableView.delegate as? ItemListDataProvider)
}
```

Run the tests. All the tests pass. This is already implemented.

Implementing ItemListDataProvider

In the previous section, we created a class to act as the data source and delegate for the item list table view. In this section, we will implement its properties and methods, but we first need a test case class for `ItemListDataProvider`.

Conducting the first tests

Open Project Navigator and select the **ToDoTests** group. Add a new **Unit Test Case Class** and call it `ItemListDataProviderTests`. Add the `@testable import ToDo` import statement and remove the two test template methods.

The table view should have two sections--one for unchecked to-do items and the other for checked items. Add the following test to `ItemListDataProviderTests`:

```
func test_NumberOfSections_IsTwo() {
    let sut = ItemListDataProvider()
    let tableView = UITableView()
    tableView.dataSource = sut

    let numberOfSections = tableView.numberOfSections
    XCTAssertEqual(numberOfSections, 2)
}
```

First, we create an instance of `ItemListDataProvider`, set up the table view, and then we check whether the table view has the expected number of sections. This test fails because the default number of sections for a table view is one. Open `ItemListDataProvider` and add the following code:

```
func numberOfSections(
    in tableView: UITableView) -> Int {


    return 2
}
```

This is enough to make all the tests pass again.

The number of rows in the first section should be the same as the number of to-do items. But where do we get the to-do items from? `ItemListDataProvider` needs a property of the type `ItemManager` to ask it for the items to present in the table view. Add the following code to `ItemListDataProviderTests`:

```
func test_NumberOfRows_Section1_IsToDoCount() {
    let sut = ItemListDataProvider()
    let tableView = UITableView()
    tableView.dataSource = sut

    sut.itemManager?.add(ToDoItem(title: "Foo"))
}
```

At this point, we have to stop writing this test because the static analyzer complains `'ItemListDataProvider'` `has` `no` `member` `'itemManager'`. Open `ItemListDataProvider` and add the property `var` `itemManager:` `ItemManager?`. This makes the test compilable again. Add the following code at the end of `test_NumberOfRows_InFirstSection_IsToDoCount()`:

```
XCTAssertEqual(tableView.numberOfRows(inSection: 0), 1)

sut.itemManager?.add(ToDoItem(title: "Bar"))

XCTAssertEqual(tableView.numberOfRows(inSection: 0), 2)
```

First, we check whether the number of rows in the first section is equal to one after we have added an item to the item manager. Then, we add another item and check whether the number of rows is equal to two. Run the test. This test fails because the number of rows in the table view is always zero, as we have not implemented the corresponding data source method to return the correct values. Open `ItemListDataProvider` and replace `tableView(_:numberOfRowsInSection:)` with the following code:

```
func tableView(_ tableView: UITableView,
               numberOfRowsInSection section: Int) -> Int {

    return itemManager?.toDoCount ?? 0
}
```

This implementation returns the number of to-do items from `itemManager` if `itemManager` is not `nil`; otherwise, it returns zero. Run the tests. Oh, they still fail because the number of rows in the first section is always zero.

The reason for this is that the property required to hold a reference to the item manager is optional, and we never set a value for this property. Therefore, the value of `itemManager` is always `nil`, and the number of rows returned from the data source method is always zero.

At this point, it is not clear who is going to set the item manager to `itemManager`. We will decide this in a later chapter when we put all the modules together to form a complete app. For the tests, we will set `itemManager` in them. Add the following line right after `let` `sut` `= ItemListDataProvider()` in `test_NumberOfRows_InFirstSection_IsToDoCount()`:

```
sut.itemManager = ItemManager()
```

Run the tests. Now the first assertion passes but the second one, asserting that the number of rows is two after we added another item, fails. The reason for this is that table views seem to cache the values returned from `tableView(_:numberOfRowsInSection:)`. This is one of the many performance optimizations that are built into table views. We, as developers, need to tell the table view that the data source has changed by calling `reloadData()`. Add the following code right after the line where the second to-do item is added to the item manager:

```
tableView.reloadData()
```

Run the tests. All the tests pass. Before we move on, let's check whether there is anything to refactor. The implementation code looks nice and clean now, but the tests show some duplication. To refactor, let's first add two properties to `ItemListDataProviderTests`:

```
var sut: ItemListDataProvider!
var tableView: UITableView!
```

Then, add the following setup code to `setUp()`:

```
sut = ItemListDataProvider()
sut.itemManager = ItemManager()


tableView = UITableView()
tableView.dataSource = sut
```

Finally, remove the following code from the test methods because it is no longer needed:

```
let sut = ItemListDataProvider()
sut.itemManager = ItemManager()

let tableView = UITableView()
tableView.dataSource = sut
```

Run the tests again to make sure that everything still works.

If the user checks an item in the first section, it should appear in the second section. Add the following test to make sure the number of rows in the second section is the same as the number of completed items in the item manager:

```
func test_NumberOfRows_Section2_IsToDoneCount() {
    sut.itemManager?.add(ToDoItem(title: "Foo"))
    sut.itemManager?.add(ToDoItem(title: "Bar"))
    sut.itemManager?.checkItem(at: 0)

    XCTAssertEqual(tableView.numberOfRows(inSection: 1), 1)
```

```
    sut.itemManager?.checkItem(at: 0)
    tableView.reloadData()

    XCTAssertEqual(tableView.numberOfRows(inSection: 1), 2)
}
```

This test is similar to the earlier test. First, we add items to the item manager, and then we check an item and see whether the number of rows in the second section matches our expectations. Run the test. The test fails but look closely: the first assertion passes. This is because the implementation of `tableView(_:numberOfRowsInSection:)` returns the number of to-do items, and when the first assertion is called this is the same as the expected number of done items. This example shows that it is important to start with a failing test, otherwise, we cannot be sure we are testing the real thing. So, remove the second assertion and make the test red by replacing `tableView(_:numberOfRowsInSection:)` with the following code:

```
func tableView(_ tableView: UITableView,
               numberOfRowsInSection section: Int) -> Int {

    let numberOfRows: Int
    switch section {
    case 0:
      numberOfRows = itemManager?.toDoCount ?? 0
    case 1:
      numberOfRows = 0
    default:
      numberOfRows = 0
    }
    return numberOfRows
}
```

Run the tests. Now, the assertion fails because the number of rows in the second section is always zero. To make the test pass, replace the assignment in `case 1` with the following line of code:

```
numberOfRows = 1
```

Run the tests again. The tests pass. Now, add the `XCTAssertEqual(tableView.numberOfRows(inSection: 1), 2)` assertion at the end of `test_NumberOfRows_InSecondSection_IsToDoneCount()` again. The test fails again. This is a good thing, however, because it means that we are actually testing whether the number of rows represents the number of items in the item manager. Replace the assignment in `case 1` one more time with the following line of code:

```
numberOfRows = itemManager?.doneCount ?? 0
```

Run the tests again. All the tests pass. Let's now check whether there is something to refactor; indeed, there is. The implementation does not look good. There is a question mark at the end of `itemManager`, and in the `switch` statement, we need to implement the `default` case even though we know that there will never be more than two sections.

To improve the code, we start by adding an enum for the sections. Add the following code in `ItemListDataProvider.swift` but outside the `ItemListDataProvider` class:

```
enum Section: Int {
    case toDo
    case done
}
```

Now, replace the implementation of `tableView(_:numberOfRowsInSection:)` with the following code:

```
func tableView(_ tableView: UITableView,
               numberOfRowsInSection section: Int) -> Int {

    guard let itemManager = itemManager else { return 0 }
    guard let itemSection = Section(rawValue: section) else {
        fatalError()
    }

    let numberOfRows: Int

    switch itemSection {
    case .toDo:
        numberOfRows = itemManager.toDoCount
    case .done:
        numberOfRows = itemManager.doneCount
    }
    return numberOfRows
}
```

This looks much better. We first check whether `itemManager` is `nil` using `guard` and return zero if this is the case. Then, we create `itemSection` from the argument `section`. The `guard` statement makes it clear that a value for the `section` argument can only be 0 or 1 because the `Section` enum only has two cases.

Run the tests to make sure that everything still works.

The to-do items should be presented in the table view using a custom table view cell because the cells provided by UIKit can only show an image and two text strings. In our case, we need to show three text strings because we want to show the title, location, and the due date.

Add the following test to make sure that `tableView(_:cellForRowAt:)` returns our custom cell:

```
func test_CellForRow_ReturnsItemCell() {
  sut.itemManager?.add(ToDoItem(title: "Foo"))
  tableView.reloadData()

  let cell = tableView.cellForRow(at: IndexPath(row: 0,
                                               section: 0))

  XCTAssertTrue(cell is ItemCell)
}
```

Xcode complains that `ItemCell` is an undeclared type. Open Project Navigator, add an **iOS | Source | Cocoa Touch Class**, and call it `ItemCell`. Make it a subclass of `UITableViewCell`. Store it in the `Controller` folder, and ensure that it is added to the **ToDo** target and not to the **ToDoTests** target. Remove all the template code, such that the file looks as follows:

```
import UIKit


class ItemCell: UITableViewCell {
}
```

Now, the test compiles but still fails. Replace the `return` statement in `tableView(_:cellForRowAt:)` with the following line of code:

```
return ItemCell()
```

This change is enough to make the tests pass, but it is clearly not enough for the feature that we want to implement. For performance reasons, table view cells need to be dequeued. Before we can write a test that makes sure that a cell is dequeued, we need to introduce a very important concept in unit testing--**fake objects**.

Fake objects

Ideally, a unit test should test one microfeature and nothing else. However, in **object-oriented programming** (OOP), objects talk to each other, exchange data, and react to the changes of their neighbors. As a result, when writing a test, it is often difficult to isolate one specific module from another. Without isolation, a test does not test just one microfeature, but many.

To isolate modules from each other, we can use a concept called fake objects. Fake objects act as placeholders for real objects or modules, but they are controlled by test code. This means a test sets up fake objects, controls their behavior, and tests whether the system under the test reacts as expected.

The most important fake objects are mocks, stubs, and fakes. These are explained as follows:

- **Mocks**: They act as recorders. They register whether the system under a test calls the expected methods of another instance with expected arguments. For example, if we have class A that should call method b() of class B, when something happens, we would create a mock for B that sets a Boolean value to true in case b() is called. In the test, we use this Boolean value to assert whether b() has been called.
- **Stubs**: These are used when we need defined return values from a method. In a test, it is often useful to have a fixed hardcoded return value for a method that the system under the test calls. The test then asserts that the system under test reacts in an expected way to the defined return value. This makes it easy to test many different scenarios without complicated setups.
- **Fakes**: They act as stand-ins for real objects that a system under test communicates with. They are needed to make the code compile, but they are not needed to assert that something expected has happened. Fakes are often used when they are easier to set up than the real objects, or when we need to make sure that the test is independent of the implementation of the real object.

For the next test, we will need a table view mock.

Using mocks

As mentioned in the previous section, table view cells should be dequeued. To make sure that this happens, we need a test. The dequeuing is done by calling the `dequeueReusableCell(withIdentifier:for:)` method on the table view. The table view then checks whether there is a cell that can be reused. If not, it creates a new cell and returns it. We are going to use a table view mock to register when the method is called.

In Swift, classes can be defined within other classes. In the case of mocks, this is useful because, this way, the mocks are only visible and accessible at the point where they are needed.

Add the following code to `ItemListDataProviderTests.swift`, outside of the `ItemListDataProviderTests` class:

```
extension ItemListDataProviderTests {
  class MockTableView: UITableView {
    var cellGotDequeued = false

    override func dequeueReusableCell(
      withIdentifier identifier: String,
      for indexPath: IndexPath) -> UITableViewCell {

      cellGotDequeued = true

      return super.dequeueReusableCell(withIdentifier: identifier,
                                       for: indexPath)
    }
  }
}
```

We have used an extension of `ItemListDataProviderTests` to define a mock of `UITableView`. Our mock uses a Boolean property to register when `dequeueReusableCell(withIdentifier:for:)` is called.

Add the following test to `ItemListDataProviderTests`:

```
func test_CellForRow_DequeuesCellFromTableView() {
  let mockTableView = MockTableView()
  mockTableView.dataSource = sut
  mockTableView.register(ItemCell.self,
                         forCellReuseIdentifier: "ItemCell")

  sut.itemManager?.add(ToDoItem(title: "Foo"))
  mockTableView.reloadData()

  _ = mockTableView.cellForRow(at: IndexPath(row: 0, section: 0))

  XCTAssertTrue(mockTableView.cellGotDequeued)
}
```

In the test, we first create an instance and set up our table view mock. Then, we add an item to the item manager of `sut`. Next, we call `cellForRow(at:)` to trigger the method call that we want to test. Finally, we assert that the table view cell is dequeued.

Run this test. It fails because the cell has not yet been dequeued. Replace the implementation of `tableView(_:cellForRowAt:)` with the following code:

```
func tableView(_ tableView: UITableView,
```

```
                cellForRowAt indexPath: IndexPath) -> UITableViewCell {

    let cell = tableView.dequeueReusableCell(
        withIdentifier: "ItemCell",
        for: indexPath)

    return cell
}
```

Run the tests. Now, the last added test succeeds, but `test_CellForRow_ReturnsItemCell()` fails. The reason for this is that we need to register a cell when we want to make use of the automatic dequeuing of cells in `UITableView`. There are three ways to register a cell. Firstly, we can do this in code, just as we did in `test_CellForRow_DequeuesCellFromTableView()`. Secondly, we can do this by registering a `nib` for the cell. Thirdly, it can be done by adding a cell with the used reuse identifier to the storyboard. We will implement the third way because we are already using a storyboard for the app.

Open `Main.storyboard` in the editor and add a **Table View Cell** to the **Table View**:

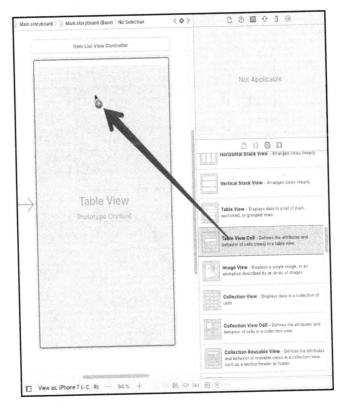

In the Identity Inspector, change the class of the cell to `ItemCell`:

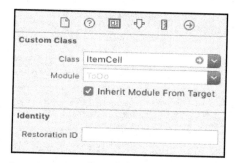

In the Attribute Inspector, set **Identifier** to `ItemCell`:

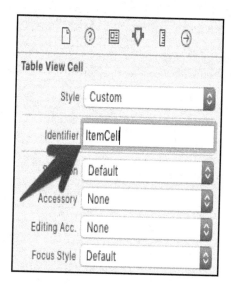

Next, we need to set up the test case such that it uses the storyboard to create the table view. First, add the following property to `ItemListDataProviderTests`:

```
var controller: ItemListViewController!
```

Then, replace `setUp()` with the following code:

```
override func setUp() {
    super.setUp()

    sut = ItemListDataProvider()
    sut.itemManager = ItemManager()
```

```
let storyboard = UIStoryboard(name: "Main", bundle: nil)
controller = storyboard.instantiateViewController(
   withIdentifier: "ItemListViewController") as!
                    ItemListViewController

controller.loadViewIfNeeded()

tableView = controller.tableView
tableView.dataSource = sut
}
```

Instead of creating a table view using an `UITableView` initializer, we instantiate an instance of `ItemListViewController` from the storyboard and use its table view. The `controller.loadViewIfNeeded()` call is needed because, otherwise, the table view is nil.

Run the tests. All the tests pass and there should be nothing to refactor.

After the cell is dequeued, the name, location, and due date should be set to labels in the cell. A common pattern in the implementation of table view cells in iOS is to implement a `configCell(with:)` method in the cell class. The table view data source then needs to call this method in `tableView(_:cellForRowAt:)`.

To make sure that `configCell(with:)` is called after the cell is dequeued, we will write a test that uses a table view cell mock. Add the following mock class after the table view mock:

```
class MockItemCell : ItemCell {
  var configCellGotCalled = false

  func configCell(with item: ToDoItem) {
    configCellGotCalled = true
  }
}
```

The mock registers when `configCell(with:)` is called by setting `configCellGotCalled` to `true`. Add the following test to `ItemListDataProviderTests`:

```
func test_CellForRow_CallsConfigCell() {

  let mockTableView = MockTableView()
  mockTableView.dataSource = sut
  mockTableView.register(
    MockItemCell.self,
    forCellReuseIdentifier: "ItemCell")
```

```
let item = ToDoItem(title: "Foo")
sut.itemManager?.add(item)
mockTableView.reloadData()

let cell = mockTableView
    .cellForRow(at: IndexPath(row: 0, section: 0)) as! MockItemCell

XCTAssertTrue(cell.configCellGotCalled)
}
```

In this test, we use a mock for the table view and for the table view cell. After setting up the table view, we add an item to the item manager. Then, we get the first cell of the table view. This triggers the call of `tableView(_:cellForRowAt:)`. Finally, we assert that `configCellGotCalled` of our table view cell mock is `true`.

Run the tests to make sure that this test fails. A failing test means that we need to write the implementation code.

Add the following line to `tableView(_:cellForRowAt:)` before the cell is returned:

```
cell.configCell(with: ToDoItem(title: ""))
```

The static analyzer will complain `'UITableViewCell' has no member 'configCell'`. Obviously, we have forgotten to cast the cell to `ItemCell`. Add the cast at the end of the line where the cell is dequeued as follows:

```
let cell = tableView.dequeueReusableCell(
    withIdentifier: "ItemCell",
    for: indexPath) as! ItemCell
```

Now, the static analyzer complains `'ItemCell' has no member 'configCell'`. Open `ItemCell.swift` and add the following empty method definition to `ItemCell`:

```
func configCell(with item: ToDoItem) {
}
```

Run the tests. Xcode complains in `MockItemCell` that `configCell(with:)` needs the `override` keyword. In Swift, whenever you override a method of the superclass, you need to add this keyword. This is a safety feature. In Objective-C, you may accidentally override a method because if you don't know that the method was defined in the superclass. This is not possible in Swift.

Add the keyword to the method definition, such that it looks like this:

```
override func configCell(with item: ToDoItem) {
  configCellGotCalled = true
}
```

Now run the tests. All the tests are green again.

Let's check whether there is something to refactor. Currently, the test_CellForRow_CallsConfigCell() test, just asserts that the method is called, but we can do better. The configCell(with:) method gets called with an item as a parameter. This item should be used to fill the label of the cell. We'll extend the test to also test whether the method is called with the expected item.

Replace the table view cell mock with the following code:

```
class MockItemCell : ItemCell {
  var catchedItem: ToDoItem?

  override func configCell(with item: ToDoItem) {
    catchedItem = item
  }
}
```

Then, replace the assertion in test_CellForRow_CallsConfigCell() with this line of code:

```
XCTAssertEqual(cell.catchedItem, item)
```

The test now fails because we have not yet used the item from the item manager. Replace tableView(_:cellForRowAt:) with the following code:

```
func tableView(_ tableView: UITableView,
               cellForRowAt indexPath: IndexPath) -> UITableViewCell {

  let cell = tableView.dequeueReusableCell(
    withIdentifier: "ItemCell",
    for: indexPath) as! ItemCell

  if let item = itemManager?.item(at: indexPath.row) {
    cell.configCell(with: item)
  }

  return cell
}
```

After dequeuing the cell, we get `toDoItem` from the item manager; call `configCell(with:)` if it succeeds.

Run the tests. All the tests pass. We are now confident that the cell is called with the right to-do item to configure its labels.

Earlier in this chapter, we tested that the number of rows in the first section corresponds to the number of unchecked to-do items, as well as the number of rows in the second section to the number of checked to-do items. Now, we need to test that the configuration of the cell in the second section passes a checked item to the configuration method.

Add the following test to `ItemListDataProviderTests`:

```
func test_CellForRow_Section2_CallsConfigCellWithDoneItem() {

    let mockTableView = MockTableView()
    mockTableView.dataSource = sut
    mockTableView.register(MockItemCell.self,
                           forCellReuseIdentifier: "ItemCell")

    sut.itemManager?.add(ToDoItem(title: "Foo"))

    let second = ToDoItem(title: "Bar")
    sut.itemManager?.add(second)
    sut.itemManager?.checkItem(at: 1)
    mockTableView.reloadData()

    let cell = mockTableView
        .cellForRow(at: IndexPath(row: 0, section: 1)) as! MockItemCell

    XCTAssertEqual(cell.catchedItem, second)
}
```

The test is similar to the earlier one. The main difference here is that we add two to-do items to the item manager and check the second to populate the second section of the table view.

Run the test. The test crashes because the runtime `unexpectedly found nil while unwrapping an Optional value`. This is strange because the similar code has worked before this. The reason for this crash is that UIKit optimizes the second section because the table view has a frame of `CGRect.zero`. As a result, `cellForRow(at:)` returns `nil`, and the `as!` forced unwrapping lets the runtime crash.

Replace the definition of the table view mock in the test with the following code:

```
let mockTableView = MockTableView(
    frame: CGRect(x: 0, y:0, width: 320, height: 480),
    style: .plain)
```

Run the tests again. It doesn't crash anymore but the test fails so, we need to write some implementation code.

In the implementation of `tableView(_:numberOfRowsInSection:)`, we introduced an enum for the table view sections, which has improved the code a lot. We will take advantage of the enum in the implementation of `tableView(_:cellForRowAt:)`. Replace the code of `tableView(_:cellForRowAt:)` with the following code:

```
func tableView(_ tableView: UITableView,
               cellForRowAt indexPath: IndexPath) -> UITableViewCell {

    let cell = tableView.dequeueReusableCell(
        withIdentifier: "ItemCell",
        for: indexPath) as! ItemCell

    guard let itemManager = itemManager else { fatalError() }
    guard let section = Section(rawValue: indexPath.section) else
    {
        fatalError()
    }

    let item: ToDoItem
    switch section {
    case .toDo:
        item = itemManager.item(at: indexPath.row)
    case .done:
        item = itemManager.doneItem(at: indexPath.row)
    }

    cell.configCell(with: item)


    return cell
}
```

After dequeuing the cell, we use `guard` to make sure that the item manager is present and the index path section has a supported value. Then, we switch on the section and assign a to-do item to a constant that is used to configure the cell. Finally, the cell is returned.

Run the tests. All the tests pass.

Look at the previous tests that you have written. They have duplicated code. Let's clean it up a bit. Add the following code to `MockTableView`:

```
class func mockTableView(
    withDataSource dataSource: UITableViewDataSource)
    -> MockTableView {

    let mockTableView = MockTableView(
        frame: CGRect(x: 0, y: 0, width: 320, height: 480),
        style: .plain)

    mockTableView.dataSource = dataSource
    mockTableView.register(MockItemCell.self,
                           forCellReuseIdentifier: "ItemCell")

    return mockTableView
}
```

This class method creates a mock table view, sets the data source, and registers the mock table view cell.

Now, we can replace the initialization and setup of the mock table view in `test_CellForRow_DequeuesCellFromTableView()`, `test_CellForRow_CallsConfigCell()`, and `test_CellForRow_InSectionTwo_CallsConfigCellWithDoneItem()` with the following:

```
let mockTableView = MockTableView.mockTableView(withDataSource: sut)
```

Run the tests to make sure that everything still works.

When a table view allows the deletion of cells and a user swipes on a cell to the left, then on the right-hand side, a red button will appear with the **Delete** title. In our application, we want to use this button to check and uncheck items. The button title should show the actions that the button is going to perform. Let's write a test to make sure that this is the case for the first section:

```
func test_DeleteButton_InFirstSection_ShowsTitleCheck() {
    let deleteButtonTitle = tableView.delegate?.tableView?(
        tableView,
        titleForDeleteConfirmationButtonForRowAt: IndexPath(row: 0,
                                                            section: 0))

    XCTAssertEqual(deleteButtonTitle, "Check")
}
```

This method is defined in the `UITableViewDelegate` protocol. Add the following line to `setUp()` right after `tableView.dataSource = sut`:

```
tableView.delegate = sut
```

The static analyzer complains that `ItemListDataProvider` does not conform to `UITableViewDelegate`. Add the conformance to it like this:

```
class ItemListDataProvider: NSObject, UITableViewDataSource,
UITableViewDelegate {
  // ...
}
```

Run the tests. The tests fail. In `ItemListDataProvider`, add the method as follows:

```
func tableView(
    _ tableView: UITableView,
    titleForDeleteConfirmationButtonForRowAt indexPath:
    IndexPath) -> String? {

    return "Check"
}
```

Now, the tests pass.

In the second section, the title of the **Delete** button should be **Uncheck**. Add the following test to `ItemListDataProviderTests`:

```
func test_DeleteButton_InSecondSection_ShowsTitleUncheck() {
    let deleteButtonTitle = tableView.delegate?.tableView?(
        tableView,
        titleForDeleteConfirmationButtonForRowAt: IndexPath(row: 0,
                                                  section: 1))

    XCTAssertEqual(deleteButtonTitle, "Uncheck")
}
```

Run the tests. The last test fails because of a missing implementation. Replace `tableView(_:titleForDeleteConfirmationButtonForRowAt:)` with this:

```
func tableView(
    _ tableView: UITableView,
    titleForDeleteConfirmationButtonForRowAt indexPath:
    IndexPath) -> String? {

    guard let section = Section(rawValue: indexPath.section) else
    {
        fatalError()
```

```
    }

    let buttonTitle: String
    switch section {
    case .toDo:
      buttonTitle = "Check"
    case .done:
      buttonTitle = "Uncheck"
    }

    return buttonTitle
  }
```

Here, we used `guard` again, as well as the `Section` enum to make the code clean and easy to read.

Run the tests. All the tests pass.

Checking and unchecking items

The last thing we need to make sure in `ItemListDataProvider` is that we can check and uncheck items and that they can then change sections. Unfortunately, like in the last test, we need to invoke the responsible data source method directly in the test. We would like to have some kind of high-level method to call to simulate the user tapping the **Check** and **Uncheck** buttons, such as in `numberOfRows(inSection:)`, but UIKit does not provide these. We will see how to use UI tests to simulate the taps of the user later in the book. Here, we will use the data source method to do this. Add the following test to `ItemListDataProviderTests`:

```
func test_CheckingAnItem_ChecksItInTheItemManager() {
  sut.itemManager?.add(ToDoItem(title: "Foo"))

  tableView.dataSource?.tableView?(tableView,
                      commit: .delete,
                      forRowAt: IndexPath(row: 0,
                                           section: 0))

  XCTAssertEqual(sut.itemManager?.toDoCount, 0)
  XCTAssertEqual(sut.itemManager?.doneCount, 1)
  XCTAssertEqual(tableView.numberOfRows(inSection: 0), 0)
  XCTAssertEqual(tableView.numberOfRows(inSection: 1), 1)
}
```

This test fails because we have not implemented `tableView(_:commit:forRowAt:)` yet. Add the following code to `ItemListDataProvider`:

```
func tableView(_ tableView: UITableView,
               commit editingStyle: UITableViewCellEditingStyle,
               forRowAt indexPath: IndexPath) {

    itemManager?.checkItem(at: indexPath.row)
    tableView.reloadData()
}
```

Run the tests. All the tests pass and there is nothing to refactor.

Next, we need to write a test for the unchecking of a to-do item. Add the following test to `ItemListDataProviderTests`:

```
func test_UncheckingAnItem_UnchecksItInTheItemManager() {

    sut.itemManager?.add(ToDoItem(title: "First"))
    sut.itemManager?.checkItem(at: 0)
    tableView.reloadData()
    tableView.dataSource?.tableView?(tableView,
                                     commit: .delete,
                                     forRowAt: IndexPath(row: 0,
                                                         section: 1))

    XCTAssertEqual(sut.itemManager?.toDoCount, 1)
    XCTAssertEqual(sut.itemManager?.doneCount, 0)
    XCTAssertEqual(tableView.numberOfRows(inSection: 0), 1)
    XCTAssertEqual(tableView.numberOfRows(inSection: 1), 0)
}
```

This test results in a crash because the code in `tableView(_:commit:forRowAt:)` tries to remove an item for the unchecked items, but the corresponding array in the item manager is already empty. Replace the implementation of `tableView(_:commit:forRowAt:)` with the following code:

```
func tableView(_ tableView: UITableView,
               commit editingStyle: UITableViewCellEditingStyle,
               forRowAt indexPath: IndexPath) {

    guard let itemManager = itemManager else { fatalError() }
    guard let section = Section(rawValue: indexPath.section) else
    {
        fatalError()
    }
```

```
  switch section {
  case .toDo:
    itemManager.checkItem(at: indexPath.row)
  case .done:
    itemManager.uncheckItem(at: indexPath.row)
  }
  tableView.reloadData()
}
```

This implementation code results in a message from the static analyzer saying `'ItemManager'` has no member `'uncheckItemAtIndex'`. It looks like we forgot to add it in the previous chapter so, let's add it now. Add the following method to `ItemManager`:

```
func uncheckItem(at index: Int) {
  let item = doneItems.remove(at: index)
  toDoItems.append(item)
}
```

Run the tests. All the tests pass and there is nothing to refactor.

Implementing ItemCell

We have tests that make sure that `configCell(with:)` gets called when the cell is prepared. Now, we need tests to make sure that the information is set to the label of `ItemCell`. You may ask, "What label?", which would be correct, as we also need tests to make sure that `ItemCell` has labels in order to present the information.

Select the **ToDoTests** group in the Project Navigator and add a new test case. Call it `ItemCellTests`. Add the import `@testable import ToDo` statement and remove the two template test methods.

To be able to present the data on the screen, `ItemCell` needs labels. We will add the labels in **Interface Builder** (**IB**). This means that to test whether the label is set up when the table view cell is loaded, we need to set up the loading in a similar way to how it will be in the app. The table view needs a data source, but we don't want to set up the real data source, because we will then need an item manager. Instead, we will use a fake object to act as the data source.

Add the following code to `ItemCellTests.swift` but outside of the `ItemCellTests` class:

```swift
extension ItemCellTests {
  class FakeDataSource: NSObject, UITableViewDataSource {

    func tableView(_ tableView: UITableView,
                   numberOfRowsInSection section: Int) -> Int {

      return 1
    }

    func tableView(_ tableView: UITableView,
                   cellForRowAt indexPath: IndexPath)
      -> UITableViewCell {

      return UITableViewCell()
    }
  }
}
```

This is the minimal implementation a table-view data source needs. Note that we are returning a plain `UITableViewCell`. We will see in a minute why this does not matter. Add the following test to `ItemCellTests`:

```swift
func test_HasNameLabel() {
    let storyboard = UIStoryboard(name: "Main", bundle: nil)
    let controller = storyboard
        .instantiateViewController(withIdentifier: "ItemListViewController")
        as! ItemListViewController

    controller.loadViewIfNeeded()

    let tableView = controller.tableView
    let dataSource = FakeDataSource()
    tableView?.dataSource = dataSource

    let cell = tableView?.dequeueReusableCell(
        withIdentifier: "ItemCell",
        for: IndexPath(row: 0, section: 0)) as! ItemCell

    XCTAssertNotNil(cell.titleLabel)
}
```

This code creates an instance of the **View Controller** from the storyboard, and it sets an instance of `FakeDataSource` to its table-view data source. Then, it dequeues a cell from the table view and asserts that this cell has `titleLabel`. This code does not compile because `'ItemCell' has no member 'titleLabel'`. Open `ItemCell.swift` in Assistant Editor and add the property declaration `let titleLabel = UILabel()`.

Run the tests. All tests pass, but the code is clearly not what we want. First, the label is not set in the storyboard and second, the label is not added to the content view of the cell. This means that when we run the app, the label isn't visible. To drive the implementation, we need a failing test.

Change the assertion in `test_HasNameLabel()` to the following:

```
XCTAssertTrue(cell.titleLabel.isDescendant(of: cell.contentView))
```

With this assertion, we check whether the `titleLabel` is added to the content view of the cell as a subview.

To make the test pass (and use the storyboard to add the label), replace the property definition `let titleLabel = UILabel()` with the declaration `@IBOutlet var titleLabel: UILabel!`.

Open `Main.storyboard` and add a label to `ItemCell` as follows:

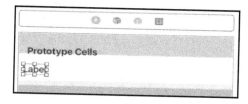

Open `ItemCell.swift` in Assistant Editor and hold down the *ctrl* key while you drag from the **Label** to the property to connect the two.

Run the tests. Now, all the tests pass.

The item cell also needs to show the location if one is set. Add the following test to `ItemCellTests`:

```
func test_HasLocationLabel() {
    let storyboard = UIStoryboard(name: "Main", bundle: nil)
    let controller = storyboard
      .instantiateViewController(
        withIdentifier:"ItemListViewController")
      as! ItemListViewController
```

```
controller.loadViewIfNeeded()

let tableView = controller.tableView
let dataSource = FakeDataSource()
tableView?.dataSource = dataSource

let cell = tableView?.dequeueReusableCell(
    withIdentifier: "ItemCell",
    for: IndexPath(row: 0, section: 0)) as! ItemCell

XCTAssertTrue(cell.locationLabel.isDescendant(of: cell.contentView))
}
```

To make this test pass, we need to perform the same steps as we did for the `Title` label. Add the `@IBOutlet var locationLabel: UILabel!` property to `ItemCell`, add `UILabel` to the cell in `Main.storyboard`, and connect the two by control-dragging from IB to the property.

Run the tests. All the tests pass, but there is a lot of duplication in the previous two tests. We need to refactor them. First, add the following properties to `ItemCellTests`:

```
var tableView: UITableView!
let dataSource = FakeDataSource()
var cell: ItemCell!
```

Then, add the following code to the end of `setUp()`:

```
let storyboard = UIStoryboard(name: "Main", bundle: nil)
let controller = storyboard
    .instantiateViewController(
        withIdentifier: "ItemListViewController")
    as! ItemListViewController

controller.loadViewIfNeeded()

tableView = controller.tableView
tableView?.dataSource = dataSource

cell = tableView?.dequeueReusableCell(
    withIdentifier: "ItemCell",
    for: IndexPath(row: 0, section: 0)) as! ItemCell
```

Remove the following code from the two test methods:

```
let storyboard = UIStoryboard(name: "Main", bundle: nil)
let controller = storyboard
  .instantiateViewController(
    withIdentifier: "ItemListViewController")
  as! ItemListViewController


_ = controller.view


let tableView = controller.tableView
let dataSource = FakeDataSource()
tableView?.dataSource = dataSource


let cell = tableView?.dequeueReusableCell(
    withIdentifier: "ItemCell",
    for: IndexPath(row: 0, section: 0)) as! ItemCell
```

Run the tests to make sure that everything still works.

We need a third label. The steps are exactly the same as those in the last tests. Make the changes yourself (don't forget the test) and call the label `dateLabel`.

Now that we have the labels in the item cell, we need to fill them with information when the cell is configured. Add the following test to `ItemCellTests`:

```
func test_ConfigCell_SetsTitle() {
  cell.configCell(with: ToDoItem(title: "Foo"))


  XCTAssertEqual(cell.titleLabel.text, "Foo")
}
```

We call `configCell(with:)` on the dequeued cell from the `setUp()` method. Run the tests. The last test fails.

To make the test pass, add the following line to `configCell(with:)`:

```
titleLabel.text = item.title
```

Now, all the tests pass again and there is nothing to refactor.

Next, we move on to the `date` label. Add the following test to `ItemCellTests`:

```
func test_ConfigCell_SetsDate() {
   let dateFormatter = DateFormatter()
   dateFormatter.dateFormat = "MM/dd/yyyy"
   let date = dateFormatter.date(from: "08/27/2017")
   let timestamp = date?.timeIntervalSince1970
   cell.configCell(with: ToDoItem(title: "Foo",
                               timestamp: timestamp))
   XCTAssertEqual(cell.dateLabel.text, "08/27/2017")
}
```

This test first creates a timestamp from a `date` string and configures the cell with it, and then it asserts whether the text of the `date` label matches the expectation.

Run the tests. The last test fails because the `dateLabel` still shows the word **Label** from when we dragged it into the storyboard scene. To make the test pass, replace `configCell(with:)` with the following code:

```
func configCell(with item: ToDoItem) {

    titleLabel.text = item.title

    if let timestamp = item.timestamp {
       let date = Date(timeIntervalSince1970: timestamp)
       let dateFormatter = DateFormatter()
       dateFormatter.dateFormat = "MM/dd/yyyy"
       dateLabel.text = dateFormatter.string(from: date)
    }
}
```

Run the tests. All tests pass, but we need to refactor. It is not a good idea to create a date formatter every time `configCell(with:)` gets called because the date formatter is the same for all cells. To improve the code, add the following property to `ItemCell`:

```
lazy var dateFormatter: DateFormatter = {
   let dateFormatter = DateFormatter()
   dateFormatter.dateFormat = "MM/dd/yyyy"
   return dateFormatter
}()
```

The `lazy` keyword indicates that this property is set the first time it is accessed. Now, you can delete the local definition of the date formatter:

```
let dateFormatter = DateFormatter()
dateFormatter.dateFormat = "MM/dd/yyyy"
```

Run the tests. Everything still works.

The implementation for the `locationLabel` (with a test first) is left for you as an exercise.

From the screenshots seen in Chapter 2, *Planning and Structuring Your Test-Driven iOS App,* we know that the `title` labels of the cells with the checked items were struck through. An item itself doesn't know that it is checked. The state of an item is managed by the item manager. This means that we need a way to put the state of the item into the `configCell(with:)` method.

Add the following test to check whether the title of the label has been struck through and that the other labels are empty:

```
func test_Title_WhenItemIsChecked_IsStrokeThrough() {
    let location = Location(name: "Bar")
    let item = ToDoItem(title: "Foo",
                        itemDescription: nil,
                        timestamp: 1456150025,
                        location: location)

    cell.configCell(with: item, checked: true)

    let attributedString = NSAttributedString(
        string: "Foo",
        attributes: [NSAttributedStringKey.strikethroughStyle:
            NSUnderlineStyle.styleSingle.rawValue])

    XCTAssertEqual(cell.titleLabel.attributedText, attributedString)
    XCTAssertNil(cell.locationLabel.text)
    XCTAssertNil(cell.dateLabel.text)
}
```

This test looks a bit like the previous one, but the main difference between them is that we call `configCell(with:checked:)` with an additional argument, and we assert that the `attributedText` of `titleLabel` is set to the expected attributed string.

This test does not compile. Replace the method signature of `configCell` with the following:

```
func configCell(with item: ToDoItem, checked: Bool = false) {
    // ...
}
```

Open `ItemListDataProviderTests.swift` and also change the signature of the overridden method in `MockItemCell`. Run the tests. The last test added fails. To make it pass, replace `configCell(with:checked:)` with the following code:

```swift
func configCell(with item: ToDoItem,
                checked: Bool = false) {
  if checked {
    let attributedString = NSAttributedString(
      string: item.title,
      attributes: [NSStrikethroughStyleAttributeName:
        NSUnderlineStyle.styleSingle.rawValue])
    titleLabel.attributedText = attributedString
    locationLabel.text = nil
    dateLabel.text = nil
  } else {
    titleLabel.text = item.title
    locationLabel.text = item.location?.name ?? ""
    if let timestamp = item.timestamp {
      let date = Date(timeIntervalSince1970: timestamp)
      dateLabel.text = dateFormatter.string(from: date)
    }
  }
}
```

In case `checked` is `true`, we set the attributed text to the **Title** label. Otherwise, we use the code that we had earlier. Run the tests. Everything works and there is nothing to refactor.

For now, we are finished with the to-do item list. In Chapter 6, *Putting It All Together*, we will connect the list view controller and the data source with the rest of the application.

In the remaining sections of this chapter, we will implement the other two view controllers. We won't go into as much detail as we have thus far because the tests and the implementation are similar to the ones we have already written.

Implementing DetailViewController

We start the implementation of `DetailViewController` with the creation of a test case. Select the **ToDoTests** group in Project Navigator and go to **iOS** | **Source** | **Unit Test Case Class**. Let's name it `DetailViewControllerTests`, and select the `Controller` folder as the destination location. Import the `@testable import ToDo` main module and delete the two template test methods.

Going by the screenshots we've seen in Chapter 2, *Planning and Structuring Your Test-Driven iOS App*, we know that DetailViewController needs a map view, four labels, and a button. Here, we will only show the TDD process for one label and the button. Add the following code to DetailViewControllerTests:

```
func test_HasTitleLabel() {
    let storyboard = UIStoryboard(name: "Main",
                                  bundle: nil)
    let sut = storyboard
        .instantiateViewController(
          withIdentifier: "DetailViewController")
        as! DetailViewController
}
```

At this point, we have to stop writing the test because there is no DetailViewController yet. Select the **ToDo** group in the Project Navigator and add an **iOS** | **Source** | **Cocoa Touch Class** with the name DetailViewController. Make it a subclass of UIViewController. As we did earlier, remove everything from the class except the minimal class definition:

```
import UIKit

class DetailViewController: UIViewController {
}
```

Now, add the following to the end of test_HasTitleLabel():

```
sut.loadViewIfNeeded()


let titleLabelIsSubView =
  sut.titleLabel?.isDescendant(
    of: sut.view) ?? false
XCTAssertTrue(titleLabelIsSubView)
```

The test does not compile because there is no titleLabel in DetailViewController. Add the following property to DetailViewController:

```
@IBOutlet var titleLabel: UILabel!
```

Run the tests. The last test fails with the error storyboard doesn't contain a view controller with identifier 'DetailViewController'. Let's fix this. Open Main.storyboard and add a **View Controller** to it. In the Identity Inspector, change its class and the **Storyboard ID** to DetailViewController.

Run the tests again. It still fails because the `titleLabel` property is `nil`. Again, open `Main.storyboard` and add a label to the **View Controller** scene. In the Assistant Editor, open `DetailViewController`, and connect the label in the storyboard to the outlet by holding down the *ctrl* key while you drag the label to the outlet.

Run the tests. Now, all the tests pass.

We already know that we need tests for the other labels and map view. So, let's put the setup code into `setUp()`. First, add the property `var sut: DetailViewController!` to `DetailViewControllerTests` and add the following code to `setUp()`:

```
let storyboard = UIStoryboard(name: "Main",
                                bundle: nil)

sut = storyboard
    .instantiateViewController(
        withIdentifier: "DetailViewController")
    as! DetailViewController
sut.loadViewIfNeeded()
```

Replace `test_HasTitleLabel()` with the following:

```
func test_HasTitleLabel() {
    let titleLabelIsSubView =
        sut.titleLabel?.isDescendant(
            of: sut.view) ?? false
    XCTAssertTrue(titleLabelIsSubView)
}
```

Run the tests again to make sure we didn't break anything during refactoring. Everything still works.

Add the remaining three labels using TDD.

For the map view, we need to add the **MapKit** framework. Select the project in the Project Navigator and switch on **Maps** in the **Capabilities** tab:

Add the following test to `DetailViewControllerTests`:

```
func test_HasMapView() {
    let mapViewIsSubView =
        sut.mapView?.isDescendant(
            of: sut.view) ?? false
    XCTAssertTrue(mapViewIsSubView)
}
```

To make the test pass, first import `MapKit` in `DetailViewController`:

```
import MapKit
```

Then, add the outlet `@IBOutlet var mapView: MKMapView!` and a map view element in the storyboard; connect the two (by control-dragging). Run the tests to make sure everything works.

When presenting `DetailViewController`, `ItemListViewController` needs to be able to set the item to be shown. As the user will be able to check items in the details view, we will pass the item manager plus the selected index to `DetailViewController`. We will assume that the details can only be presented for unchecked items. This makes sense for the app because checked items are no longer that important for the user. If we later decide that we also want to show the details for checked items, we can still add this feature.

We will now write a test that ensures that we can pass the data to `DetailViewController`, and that the information is shown in the labels. Add the following code to `DetailViewControllerTests`:

```
func test_SettingItemInfo_SetsTextsToLabels() {
    let coordinate = CLLocationCoordinate2DMake(51.2277, 6.7735)

    let location = Location(name: "Foo", coordinate: coordinate)
    let item = ToDoItem(title: "Bar",
                        itemDescription: "Baz",
                        timestamp: 1456150025,
                        location: location)

    let itemManager = ItemManager()
    itemManager.add(item)

    sut.itemInfo = (itemManager, 0)
}
```

There are two errors in this code already. Firstly, `CLLocationCoordinate2D(_:_:)` is defined in Core Location; we need to add this module to the test code. Add the following import statement immediately below the existing import statements:

```
import CoreLocation
```

Secondly, `'DetailViewController'` has no member `'itemInfo'`. Add the following property declaration to `DetailViewController`:

```
var itemInfo: (ItemManager, Int)?
```

With this change, there are no longer any errors from the static analyzer. Let's move on.

We will fill the labels with the information from the to-do item in `viewWillAppear(_:)`. Because of this, we need to trigger the call of that method in the test. It is not recommended that you call this method directly. Instead, you can ask **View Controller** to begin and end the appearance transition. Add the following code to `test_SettingItemInfo_SetsTextsToLabels()`:

```
sut.beginAppearanceTransition(true, animated: true)
sut.endAppearanceTransition()
XCTAssertEqual(sut.titleLabel.text, "Bar")
XCTAssertEqual(sut.dateLabel.text, "02/22/2016")
XCTAssertEqual(sut.locationLabel.text, "Foo")
XCTAssertEqual(sut.descriptionLabel.text, "Baz")
XCTAssertEqualWithAccuracy(sut.mapView.centerCoordinate.latitude,
                           coordinate.latitude,
                           accuracy: 0.001)
XCTAssertEqualWithAccuracy(sut.mapView.centerCoordinate.longitude,
                           coordinate.longitude,
                           accuracy: 0.001)
```

 Normally, you would put the tests for the different label and the map view into their own tests. We have put it into one test method here to keep the chapter short. Take your time and split the last test into several smaller tests.

With `beginAppearanceTransition(_:animated:)` and `endAppearanceTransition()`, we trigger the call of `viewWillAppear(_:)` (as well as `viewDidAppear(_:)` and similar methods for the presentation of the view hierarchy). Then, we assert that the information from the to-do item is set to the labels and map view of `DetailViewController`. Run the tests. The last test fails because we haven't implemented `viewWillAppear(_:)` yet. Open `DetailViewController` and add the implementation as follows:

```
override func viewWillAppear(_ animated: Bool) {
  super.viewWillAppear(animated)

  guard let itemInfo = itemInfo else { return }
  let item = itemInfo.0.item(at: itemInfo.1)
  titleLabel.text = item.title
  locationLabel.text = item.location?.name
  descriptionLabel.text = item.itemDescription

  if let timestamp = item.timestamp {
    let date = Date(timeIntervalSince1970: timestamp)
    dateLabel.text = dateFormatter.string(from: date)
```

```
    }

    if let coordinate = item.location?.coordinate {
        let region = MKCoordinateRegionMakeWithDistance(coordinate,
                                                         100, 100)
        mapView.region = region
    }
}
```

Add the definition of the date formatter below the existing properties:

```
let dateFormatter: DateFormatter = {
    let dateFormatter = DateFormatter()
    dateFormatter.dateFormat = "MM/dd/yyyy"
    return dateFormatter
}()
```

Run the tests. All the tests pass again and there is nothing to refactor.

Next, we need to implement the **Check** button. When the user taps the **Check** button, the item should be checked in the item manager. Add the following test to `DetailViewControllerTests`:

```
func test_CheckItem_ChecksItemInItemManager() {
    let itemManager = ItemManager()
    itemManager.add(ToDoItem(title: "Foo"))

    sut.itemInfo = (itemManager, 0)
    sut.checkItem()

    XCTAssertEqual(itemManager.toDoCount, 0)
    XCTAssertEqual(itemManager.doneCount, 1)
}
```

This test does not compile because there is no `checkItem()` method in `DetailViewController`. Add the minimal implementation to make the test compile as follows:

```
func checkItem() {
}
```

Now, the test compiles, but it fails because the method does nothing. To make the test pass, add the following code to `checkItem()`:

```
func checkItem() {
  if let itemInfo = itemInfo {
    itemInfo.0.checkItem(at: itemInfo.1)
  }
}
```

Run the tests. All the tests pass and there is nothing to refactor. Next, we need to implement `InputViewController`.

Implementing InputViewController

Add a test case with the name `InputViewControllerTests`, import the `ToDo` module, and remove the two template methods. If you have problems with this task, go back to the beginning of the previous sections, where we covered this in more detail.

You have taken a look at the first steps of the TDD of controllers several times now. Therefore, we will perform several steps at once and put the setup code directly in `setUp()`. Firstly, add the property `var sut: InputViewController!`. Secondly, add the view controller class `InputViewController`. Again, if you are unsure about how to do this, have a look at the previous sections. Next, add the following setup code to `setUp()`:

```
let storyboard = UIStoryboard(name: "Main",
                              bundle: nil)
sut = storyboard
  .instantiateViewController(
    withIdentifier: "InputViewController")
  as! InputViewController


sut.loadViewIfNeeded()
```

Add the following test:

```
func test_HasTitleTextField() {
  let titleTextFieldIsSubView =
    sut.titleTextField?.isDescendant(
      of: sut.view) ?? false
  XCTAssertTrue(titleTextFieldIsSubView)
}
```

This test does not compile because `InputViewController` does not have a member called `titleTextField`. To make the test compile, add the property `@IBOutlet var titleTextField: UITextField!` to `InputViewController`. If you run the test, it still does not pass. We already know what is needed to make it pass from the implementation of `DetailViewController`. First, add a **View Controller** to the storyboard. Change its **Class** and **Storyboard ID** to `InputViewController`. Second, add a text field to the storyboard scene and connect it to the outlet in `InputViewController`. This should be enough to make the test pass.

Now add the rest of the text fields and the two buttons (`dateTextField`, `locationTextField`, `addressTextField`, `descriptionTextField`, `saveButton`, and `cancelButton`) in a test-driven way. Make sure that all tests pass before you move on, and don't forget to refactor your code and tests if needed.

In the address field, the user can put in addresses for the to-do items. The app should then fetch the coordinate and store it in the to-do items' location. Apple provides the `CLGeocoder` class in `CoreLocation` for this task. In the test, we want to mock this class to be independent of the internet connection. Import the `CoreLocation` module (`import CoreLocation`) and add the following code to `InputViewControllerTests.swift` outside of the class `InputViewControllerTests`:

```
extension InputViewControllerTests {
  class MockGeocoder: CLGeocoder {

    var completionHandler: CLGeocodeCompletionHandler?

    override func geocodeAddressString(
      _ addressString: String,
      completionHandler: @escaping CLGeocodeCompletionHandler) {

      self.completionHandler = completionHandler
    }
  }
}
```

The only thing the mock does is capture the completion handler when `geocodeAddressString(_:completionHandler:)` is called. This way, we can call the completion handler in the test and check whether the system under the test works as expected.

The signature of the completion handler looks as follows:

```
public typealias CLGeocodeCompletionHandler = ([CLPlacemark]?, NSError?) ->
Void
```

The first argument is an optional array of place marks, which are sorted from the best to worst match. In the test, we would like to return a place mark with a defined coordinate to check whether the to-do item is created correctly. The problem is that all the properties in `CLPlacemark` are `readonly`, and it does not have an initializer that we can use to set the coordinate. Therefore, we need another mock that allows us to override the location property. Add the following class definition to the `InputViewControllerTests` extension:

```
class MockPlacemark : CLPlacemark {

  var mockCoordinate: CLLocationCoordinate2D?

  override var location: CLLocation? {
    guard let coordinate = mockCoordinate else
    { return CLLocation() }

    return CLLocation(latitude: coordinate.latitude,
                      longitude: coordinate.longitude)
  }
}
```

Now, we are ready for the test. The test is a bit complicated. To clearly show you what is going on, we will show the complete test, and then add implementation code until the test passes. By doing this, we are not following the TDD workflow, as we will get errors from the static analyzer before we have even finished writing the test method. This way also makes it easier to see what is going on. First, add a property for the place mark mock to `InputViewControllerTests`:

```
var placemark: MockPlacemark!
```

This is needed because the test would crash if the place mark is accessed outside of its definition scope. Add the following test method to `InputViewControllerTests`:

```
func test_Save_UsesGeocoderToGetCoordinateFromAddress() {
  let dateFormatter = DateFormatter()
  dateFormatter.dateFormat = "MM/dd/yyyy"

  let timestamp = 1456095600.0
  let date = Date(timeIntervalSince1970: timestamp)

  sut.titleTextField.text = "Foo"
  sut.dateTextField.text = dateFormatter.string(from: date)
  sut.locationTextField.text = "Bar"
  sut.addressTextField.text = "Infinite Loop 1, Cupertino"
  sut.descriptionTextField.text = "Baz"
```

```
let mockGeocoder = MockGeocoder()
sut.geocoder = mockGeocoder

sut.itemManager = ItemManager()

sut.save()

placemark = MockPlacemark()
let coordinate = CLLocationCoordinate2DMake(37.3316851,
                                            -122.0300674)
placemark.mockCoordinate = coordinate
mockGeocoder.completionHandler?([placemark], nil)

let item = sut.itemManager?.item(at: 0)

let testItem = ToDoItem(title: "Foo",
                        itemDescription: "Baz",
                        timestamp: timestamp,
                        location: Location(name: "Bar",
                                           coordinate: coordinate))

    XCTAssertEqual(item, testItem)
}
```

Let's take a look at what is going on here. Firstly, we create the text for the `date` text field from an arbitrary timestamp. We set the `date` text and the other text values to the text fields. Then, we create a geocoder mock and set it to a property of the `sut`. This is called a dependency injection. We inject the instance from the test that should be used to fetch the coordinate for the given address. To add an item to the list of to-do items, `InputViewController` needs to have an item manager. In the test, we set it to a new instance. Next, we call the method we want to test (`save()`). This should call `geocodeAddressString(_:completionHandler:)` of our geocoder mock, and as a result, the mock should capture the completion handler from the implementation. In the next step, we call the completion handler with a place mark that has a given coordinate. We expect that the completion handler uses the place mark and information from the text fields to create a to-do item. In the rest of the test methods, we assert that this is actually the case.

Now, let's make the test pass. `InputViewController` needs a geocoder, so import `CoreLocation` to `InputViewController` and add this property:

```
lazy var geocoder = CLGeocoder()
```

Lazy properties are set the first time they are accessed. This way, we can set our mock to `geocoder` before we access it in the test for the first time. We inject the dependency in the test. In the implementation code, we can use `geocoder` as it would be a normal property.

Next, we add a property to hold a reference to the item manager:

```
var itemManager: ItemManager?
```

To make the test compilable, add the minimal implementation of the `save` method:

```
func save() {
}
```

Now, we need to create a to-do item and add it to the item manager within `save()`. Add the following code to `save()`:

```
guard let titleString = titleTextField.text,
    titleString.characters.count > 0 else { return }
let date: Date?
if let dateText = self.dateTextField.text,
    dateText.characters.count > 0 {
    date = dateFormatter.date(from: dateText)
} else {
    date = nil
}
let descriptionString = descriptionTextField.text
if let locationName = locationTextField.text,
    locationName.characters.count > 0 {
    if let address = addressTextField.text,
        address.characters.count > 0 {

        geocoder.geocodeAddressString(address) {
            [unowned self] (placeMarks, error) -> Void in

            let placeMark = placeMarks?.first

            let item = ToDoItem(
                title: titleString,
                itemDescription: descriptionString,
                timestamp: date?.timeIntervalSince1970,
                location: Location(
                    name: locationName,
                    coordinate: placeMark?.location?.coordinate))

            self.itemManager?.add(item)
        }
    }
}
```

Let's go over the code step by step.

First, we use `guard` to get the string from the `Title` text field. If there is nothing in the field, we immediately return from the method. Next, we get the date and description of the to-do item from the corresponding text fields. The date is created from the string in the text field using a date formatter. Add the date formatter immediately above `save()`:

```
let dateFormatter: DateFormatter = {
  let dateFormatter = DateFormatter()
  dateFormatter.dateFormat = "MM/dd/yyyy"
  return dateFormatter
}()
```

Then, we check whether a name is given in the `Location` text field. If this is the case, we check whether an address is given in the `Address` text field. In this case, we get the coordinate from the `geocoder`, create the to-do item, and add it to the item manager.

Run the tests. All the tests pass and there is nothing to refactor.

The implementation of `save()` is not finished yet. The minimum input a user has to give is the title. Add tests for the to-do items with less information given by the user.

The last test for this chapter is to test that the `Save` button is connected to the `save()` action. Add the following test to `InputViewControllerTests`:

```
func test_SaveButtonHasSaveAction() {
  let saveButton: UIButton = sut.saveButton

  guard let actions = saveButton.actions(
    forTarget: sut,
    forControlEvent: .touchUpInside) else {
      XCTFail(); return
  }

  XCTAssertTrue(actions.contains("save"))
}
```

We should get the `Save` button and `guard` that it has at least one action; if not, we fail the test using `XCTFail()`. Then, we assert that the `actions` array has a method, the `"save"` selector.

Run the tests. The last test fails.

Change the signature of the `save` method to `@IBAction func save()` and connect it to the `Save` button in the storyboard scene (do this by hitting the *ctrl* key + dragging from the button in the storyboard to the `IBAction` in code).

Run the tests again. Now, all the tests pass.

Summary

In this chapter, we looked at how to implement a view controller with a table view using TDD. We split the table view controller into code that manages the view hierarchy and code for the data source, and the delegate of the table view.

We discussed how to write tests to drive the development of subviews, outlets, and actions, and how to use fake objects to isolate the microfeature to be tested. The usage of mock objects allowed us to create fast, isolated, and reliable tests. This way, we were able to write tests for the table view cell without the need to instantiate the real data source of the table view.

Next, we implemented the detail view controller using TDD. We added MapKit to the project in order to show the location of the to-do item in case a user added an address.

Finally, we wrote tests to drive the implementation of the input view controller. We also looked at how to stub an asynchronous API to make the test execution fast.

In this chapter, we set up the system under tests using the code and instantiating from a storyboard. You should now be able to use both techniques, depending on the feature you test.

In the next chapter, we will take a look at how to build the network layer of the app using TDD without a finished server side.

5
Testing Network Code

Most apps in the App Store perform networking in one way or the other. Apple provides a great class for network requests--`URLSession`. Its requests are asynchronous. This means that the response is delivered on a background thread. If that wasn't the case, the UI would freeze while the app waits for a response from the server.

The main topic of this chapter is how to test an asynchronous API. There are two ways to write tests for asynchronous API calls. First, it can be done using the real server that is going to be used when the app is in the App Store. Second, it can be done using stubs, as we did in the previous chapter.

Both methods have their advantages. Tests with the real server let us additionally test whether the server is implemented as described in the documentation. Those tests are closer to the implementation of the finished app and, therefore, are more likely to find bugs that would end up in the final version.

On the flip side, stubs let us develop the network layer of our app even before the web service is implemented. We just need the documentation of the API calls and the expected responses. As the tests do not depend on communication with a server, the test execution is significantly faster.

You should have both kinds of tests in your iOS development toolbox.

This chapter covers the following topics:

- Implementing tests using a live web service
- Implementing a login request to a fake web service
- Handling errors

Implementing tests using a web service

In the previous chapter, we wrote a stub for CLGeocoder. Now, we will write a test that asserts that the geocoder built into CoreLocation works as we expect it to. The fetching of coordinates from a geocoder is asynchronous. This means that we have to write a test that can deal with asynchronous interfaces.

Let's first structure the files a bit in the Project Navigator of Xcode. Select all the controller files in the main target (ItemListViewController.swift, ItemListDataProvider.swift, ItemCell.swift, DetailViewController.swift, and InputViewController.swift), and press *ctrl* + click to create a group from the selection. Let's call this group Controller. Do the same with the corresponding test cases in the test target.

Now, let's get started with the test. We start naively by adding the following test to InputViewControllerTests:

```swift
func test_Geocoder_FetchesCoordinates() {

  let address = "Infinite Loop 1, Cupertino"
  CLGeocoder()
    .geocodeAddressString(address) {
      (placemarks, error) -> Void in

      let coordinate =
        placemarks?.first?.location?.coordinate
        guard let latitude =
        coordinate?.latitude else {
          XCTFail()
          return
      }

      guard let longitude =
        coordinate?.longitude else {
          XCTFail()
          return
      }

      XCTAssertEqual(latitude,
                     37.3316,
                     accuracy: 0.001)
      XCTAssertEqual(longitude,
                     -122.0300,
                     accuracy: 0.001)
    }
}
```

Run the tests. All the tests pass. So, it looks like that the geocoder works as we thought it would. But wait a minute. We have skipped the red phase. In TDD, we first have to have a failing test. Otherwise, we cannot be sure whether the test actually works.

We have no access to the source of `CLGeocoder`, so we cannot change its implementation to make the test fail. The only thing we can do is to change the assertion. Replace the assertions within the closure with this code:

```
XCTAssertEqual(latitude,
               0.0,
               accuracy: 0.001)
XCTAssertEqual(longitude,
               0.0,
               accuracy: 0.001)
```

Run the tests again. Uh, the tests still pass. To figure out what is going on, add a breakpoint in the line of the first assertion:

Run the tests again. During the execution of this test, the debugger should stop at this line, so open the debugger console to investigate what is going on.

The debugger never reaches the breakpoint.

The reason for this is that `geocodeAddressString(_:completionHandler:)` call is asynchronous. This means that the closure is called sometime in the future on a different thread, and the execution of the tests moves on. The test is finished before the callback block is executed, and the assertions never get called. We need to change the test to make it asynchronous.

Replace `test_Geocoder_FetchesCoordinates()` with the following lines of code:

```
func test_Geocoder_FetchesCoordinates() {
    let geocoderAnswered = expectation(description: "Geocoder")
    let address = "Infinite Loop 1, Cupertino"
    CLGeocoder()
      .geocodeAddressString(address) {
        (placemarks, error) -> Void in

        let coordinate =
          placemarks?.first?.location?.coordinate
        guard let latitude =
          coordinate?.latitude else {
```

```
            XCTFail()
            return
     }

    guard let longitude =
      coordinate?.longitude else {


            XCTFail()
            return
     }
    XCTAssertEqual(latitude,
                  0.0,
                  accuracy: 0.001)
    XCTAssertEqual(longitude,
                  0.0,
                  accuracy: 0.001)

    geocoderAnswered.fulfill()
  }

  waitForExpectations(timeout: 3,
                      handler: nil)
  }
```

The new lines are highlighted. We create an expectation using `expectation(description:)`. At the end of the test, we call `waitForExpectations(timeout:handler:)` with a timeout of 3 seconds. This tells the test runner that it should stop at this point and wait until either all the expectations that are created in the test are fulfilled, or the timeout duration is over. If all the expectations are not fulfilled when the timeout duration has passed, the test fails. In the callback closure, we fulfill the expectation after the assertions are called.

Now, run the tests again. The last test fails because the coordinate we get from the geocoder does not match the values (`0.0` and `0.0`) we put into the assertions. Replace the assertions again with the correct ones that we had when we first wrote the test:

```
XCTAssertEqual(latitude,
               37.3316,
               accuracy: 0.001)
XCTAssertEqual(longitude,
               -122.0300,
               accuracy: 0.001)
```

Run the tests again. All the tests pass, and `CLGeocoder` works as expected.

We have just taken a look at how we can use `XCTest` to test asynchronous APIs. This can be used to test many different aspects of iOS development (for example, sending `NSNotifications`, fetching data from a web server, writing data to a database in the background, and so on). Whenever something asynchronous takes place, we can add expectations and set them as fulfilled when the asynchronous callback is executed.

This is very powerful. But keep in mind that unit tests should be fast and reliable. Using a web service in your tests makes the test fragile and slow. If the web server needs more than three seconds that we set as `timeout`, the test will fail. And you always need internet connectivity to run this test.

In the following sections, we will use stubs to make an asynchronous test robust and fast. The additional benefit is that we can develop the network layer of our app without a finished web server at hand. The only thing we need is a finished API documentation.

Implementing a login request

Let's assume that a colleague is developing a web service, but it is not finished yet. However, we already know what the API will look like. There will be an endpoint for the login. The URL will be `https://awesometodos.com/login`; it will take two parameters: a `username` and `password`, and it will return a token that has to be used with each further call to the API.

We need a test that asserts that the token that is returned from the login call is put into a token `struct`.

Add a new **iOS** | **Source** | **Unit Test Case Class**, and call it `APIClientTests`. Import the main module so that it can be tested (`@testable import ToDo`), and remove the two template tests.

We will split the login feature into several micro features. As mentioned previously, the login should make an HTTPS request to `https://awesometodos.com/login` with the `username` and `password` as query parameters. Let's write a test for this.

Add the following code to `APIClientTests`:

```
func test_Login_UsesExpectedHost() {

    let sut = APIClient()
}
```

The static analyzer tells us that we need an `APIClient` class. Add an **iOS | Source | Swift File** to the main target, and call it `APIClient.swift`. Add the following code to it:

```
class APIClient {
}
```

This is enough to make the static analyzer happy.

You need to be able to inject a fake URL session that fakes the network call because the server side isn't finished yet. Add the following code to `test_Login_UsesExpectedHost()`:

```
let mockURLSession = MockURLSession()
```

This code does not compile because the mock class is missing. Add the following code to `APIClientTests.swift`, but outside of the class definition:

```
extension APIClientTests {

  class MockURLSession {
    var url: URL?
    func dataTask(
      with url: URL,
      completionHandler: @escaping
      (Data?, URLResponse?, Error?) -> Void)
      -> URLSessionDataTask {

      self.url = url
      return URLSession.shared.dataTask(with: url)
    }
  }
}
```

This mock class implements the method `dataTask(with:completionHandler:)`, because this is the method we want to use in the implementation of the network requests. The mock class catches the URL. This enables us to check the URL in the test. Next, we want to inject the mock class into the implementation. Add the following code at the end of `test_Login_UsesExpectedHost()`:

```
sut.session = mockURLSession
```

To make this code compilable, you need to add a `session` property. Open `APIClient` and add this property:

```
lazy var session: URLSession = URLSession.shared
```

Try to run the tests. The test will still not compile. The reason for this is that it complains `cannot assign value of type 'APIClientTests.MockURLSession' to type 'URLSession'`. This makes sense. You have to change the type of `session` in order to be able to set it either as an instance of `URLSession` or an instance of our mock class. The key is to use `protocol`. Add the following code in `APIClient.swift` but outside of `APIClient`:

```
protocol SessionProtocol {
   func dataTask(
     with url: URL,
     completionHandler: @escaping
     (Data?, URLResponse?, Error?) -> Void)
     -> URLSessionDataTask
}
```

`URLSession` already implements the protocol method. To make it conform to `protocol`, add the following extension in `APIClient.swift` (but outside of the class definition):

```
extension URLSession: SessionProtocol {}
```

Next, you have to tell the compiler that the mock class conforms to that protocol as well. Change the definition of the mock class to the following one:

```
class MockURLSession: SessionProtocol {
   // ...
}
```

Finally, you have to change the type of the `session` property. In `APIClient`, replace the `URLSession` type with `SessionProtocol` like this:

```
lazy var session: SessionProtocol = URLSession.shared
```

Run the tests. Now, the test compiles, and you can continue. `APIClient` needs a method that does the login. Add the following code to `test_Login_UsesExpectedHost()`:

```
let completion = { (token: Token?, error: Error?) in }
sut.loginUser(withName:"dasdom",
              password: "1234",
              completion: completion)
```

This does not compile because of the
method `loginUser(withName:password:completion:)` and the `Token` struct are
missing. Open `APIClient`, and add the following code:

```
func loginUser(withName username: String,
               password: String,
               completion: @escaping (Token?, Error?) -> Void) {

}
```

Next, add an **iOS** | **Source** | **Swift File** to the main target and call it `Token.swift`. Add the
following code:

```
struct Token {

}
```

This is enough to make the test compilable again.

To make sure that the login method uses the expected host, add the following code at the
end of `test_Login_UsesExpectedHost()`:

```
guard let url = mockURLSession.url else { XCTFail(); return }
let urlComponents = URLComponents(url: url,
                                  resolvingAgainstBaseURL: true)
XCTAssertEqual(urlComponents?.host, "awesometodos.com")
```

This code gets the URL components from `mockURLSession` (remember that our session
mock catches the URL) and asserts that the host of the URL is `awesometodos.com`.

Run this test. It fails. To make it pass, add the following code to
`loginUser(withName:password:completion:)`:

```
guard let url = URL(string: "https://awesometodos.com") else {
    fatalError()
}
session.dataTask(with: url) { (data, response, error) in

}
```

Run the tests again. Now all the tests pass, and there is nothing to refactor. Next, let's add a
test for the path of the URL. Copy the test method `test_Login_UsesExpectedHost()`,
change the method name of the copy to `test_Login_UsesExpectedPath()` and replace
the assertion with the following:

```
XCTAssertEqual(urlComponents?.path, "/login")
```

To make the test pass again, replace the definition of the URL with this:

```
guard let url = URL(string: "https://awesometodos.com/login") else {
    fatalError()
}
```

Run the tests to make sure that all the tests pass. The two tests in `APIClientTests` share a lot of code. Let's refactor the tests to be more readable.

Add the following two properties to `APIClientTests`:

```
var sut: APIClient!
var mockURLSession: MockURLSession!
```

Next, add these lines to set up after `super.setUp()`:

```
sut = APIClient()
mockURLSession = MockURLSession()
sut.session = mockURLSession
```

With these changes, the setup of the system under test is done in `setup()`. Remove the following lines from the two test methods:

```
let sut = APIClient()
let mockURLSession = MockURLSession()
sut.session = mockURLSession
```

Run the tests. All tests still pass. But wait a minute. How do we know that the tests still work? We have changed the tests. What if we changed the tests in a way that they always pass? Sometimes it's good to be paranoid about the tests. So, let's test the tests.

In `APIClient` change the generated URL to:

```
guard let url = URL(string: "https://example.com") else {
    fatalError()
}
```

Run the tests. Both tests in `APIClientTests` fail. Good. So, they still work. Fix the code that the tests pass again.

There is still room for improvement in the tests. Before we can assert that the host and the path are as expected, we have to create an instance of URLComponents with the caught url. The test would be much cleaner if we put that code into the MockURLSession. So let's do exactly this. Add the following code to MockURLSession:

```
var urlComponents: URLComponents? {
  guard let url = url else { return nil }
  return URLComponents(url: url,
                       resolvingAgainstBaseURL: true)
}
```

Then we can replace the assertions in the test methods with this:

```
func test_Login_UsesExpectedHost() {


  // ...


  XCTAssertEqual(
    mockURLSession.urlComponents?.host,
    "awesometodos.com")
}


func test_Login_UsesExpectedPath() {

  // ...

  XCTAssertEqual(
    mockURLSession.urlComponents?.path,
    "/login")
}
```

Much better! Run the tests. All tests still pass. Now we can move on.

Next, you need to make sure that username and password are passed as parameters in the URL query. Copy the test method test_Login_UsesExpectedPath(), change the name of the copy to test_Login_UsesExpectedQuery() and replace the assertion with this:

```
XCTAssertEqual(
  mockURLSession.urlComponents?.query,
  "username=dasdom&password=1234")
```

Run this test. The test fails because you do not use `username` and `password` to construct the URL. To make the test pass, replace the URL with the following one:

```
let query = "username=\(username)&password=\(password)"
guard let url = URL(string:
    "https://awesometodos.com/login?\(query)") else {
    fatalError()
}
```

Now, the tests pass again. But if you have worked with a web service before, you might have realized that there is a problem with your code. Some characters have a special meaning when they are used in a URL. For example, the character & splits the URL query into query items. But the user could use this character in their password. We need to encode the query items. Let's change the test to drive the change of the implementation code. First, change the call of `loginUser(withName:password:completion:)` in `test_Login_UsesExpectedQuery()` to use special characters in `username` and `password`:

```
sut.loginUser(withName:"dasdöm",
              password: "%&34",
              completion: completion)
```

Next, replace the assertion for the query with the following code:

```
XCTAssertEqual(
    mockURLSession.urlComponents?
      .percentEncodedQuery,
    "username=dasd%C3%B6m&password=%25%2634")
```

With these changes, you assert that `username` and `password` are properly encoded to be used in a URL query. Note that we are now using the `percentEncodedQuery` of `URLComponents`. Go ahead, look up the difference between `query` and `percentEncodedQuery`.

Run the tests. The test crashes because you chose to call `fatalError()` in case the URL cannot be constructed for the string. To remove the crash and make the test pass, replace the contents of `loginUser(withName:password:completion:)` with the following lines of code:

```
let allowedCharacters = CharacterSet(
    charactersIn:
    "/%&=?$#+-~@<>|\\*,.()[]{}^!").inverted


guard let encodedUsername = username.addingPercentEncoding(
    withAllowedCharacters: allowedCharacters) else { fatalError() }
```

```
guard let encodedPassword = password.addingPercentEncoding(
   withAllowedCharacters: allowedCharacters) else { fatalError() }


let query = "username=\(encodedUsername)&password=\(encodedPassword)"
guard let url = URL(string:
   "https://awesometodos.com/login?\(query)") else {
   fatalError()
}


session.dataTask(with: url) { (data, response, error) in

}
```

With this code, you encode `username` and `password` before you construct the URL. Run the tests. Now, all the tests pass again.

The encoding makes the method `loginUser(withName:password:completion:)` hard to read. It would be easier to read if we could encode with code like this:

```
username.percentEncode()
```

So let's add an extension to `String`. Add the following code in `APIClient.swift`, but outside of the class `APIClient`:

```
extension String {


   var percentEncoded: String {

      let allowedCharacters = CharacterSet(
         charactersIn:
         "/%&=?$#+-~@<>|\\*,.()[]{}^!").inverted

      guard let encoded = self.addingPercentEncoding(
         withAllowedCharacters: allowedCharacters) else { fatalError() }

      return encoded
   }
}
```

With this change, we can write the
method `loginUser(withName:password:completion:)` like this:

```
func loginUser(withName username: String,
              password: String,
              completion: @escaping (Token?, Error?) -> Void)

  let query = "username=\(username.percentEncoded)&password=
(password.percentEncoded)"
    guard let url = URL(string:
      "https://awesometodos.com/login?\(query)") else {
        fatalError()
    }
    session.dataTask(with: url) { (data, response, error) in
    }
}
```

Right now the test depends on the order of the query items. This is not a good idea because in a URL, the order is irrelevant. This means the test could fail even if the URL is correct. So you should refactor the test before you proceed with the next test.

`URLComponents` has a property called `queryItems`. This should help.

Right now, `MockURLSession` only catches the URL of the request. To test the login code, we need to be able to call the completion handler of the data task in the test. This way, we can ensure that the login code processes the returned data in the way we expect. We will accomplish this task by catching the completion handler and calling it when `resume` on the `dataTask` is called.

To do this, you need to create a mock for the data task first. Add the following mock class to the extension on `APIClientTests`:

```
class MockTask: URLSessionDataTask {
    private let data: Data?
    private let urlResponse: URLResponse?
    private let responseError: Error?

    typealias CompletionHandler = (Data?, URLResponse?, Error?)
      -> Void
    var completionHandler: CompletionHandler?

    init(data: Data?, urlResponse: URLResponse?, error: Error?) {
        self.data = data
```

```
      self.urlResponse = urlResponse
      self.responseError = error
   }

   override func resume() {
     DispatchQueue.main.async() {
       self.completionHandler?(self.data,
                               self.urlResponse,
                               self.responseError)
     }
   }
 }
}
```

This code defines four properties. The first three properties are used to set the values to be fed into the completion handler. The fourth property is the completion handler to be executed when resume() gets called.

In addition, this mock has two methods: an init method that takes the values for the completion handler and the overridden resume method. In the resume method, the completion handler is dispatched to the main queue. This is done to make sure that the completion handler is asynchronous to the surrounding code.

MockURLSession has to create a mock data task and return it when dataTask(with:completionHandler:) is called. Replace the MockURLSession class with the following implementation:

```
class MockURLSession: SessionProtocol {
  var url: URL?
  private let dataTask: MockTask

  var urlComponents: URLComponents? {
    guard let url = url else { return nil }
    return URLComponents(url: url,
                         resolvingAgainstBaseURL: true)
  }
  init(data: Data?, urlResponse: URLResponse?, error: Error?) {
    dataTask = MockTask(data: data,
                        urlResponse: urlResponse,
                        error: error)
  }

  func dataTask(
    with url: URL,
    completionHandler: @escaping
    (Data?, URLResponse?, Error?) -> Void)
    -> URLSessionDataTask {
      self.url = url
```

```
            print(url)
            dataTask.completionHandler = completionHandler
            return dataTask
    }
}
```

You have added an init method to create and store the data task. The parameters in the init method take the values to be used when calling the completion handler. In `dataTask(with:completionHandler:)`, you store the completion handler in the mock data task and return the mock data task.

With all this preparation, the completion handler of the request gets executed when the resume of the mock data task is called. The parameters of the completion handler are set when an instance of `MockURLSession` is instantiated.

Because you have added an init method to the `MockURLSession` class, the initialization of the mock URL session in the previous test does not compile anymore. Replace the line `let mockURLSession = MockURLSession()` with `let mockURLSession = MockURLSession(data: nil, urlResponse: nil, error: nil)` to make it compilable again.

With these changes made, you are ready for the test. Add the following test to `APIClientTests`:

```
func test_Login_WhenSuccessful_CreatesToken() {
    let jsonData =
      "{\"token\": \"1234567890\"}"
        .data(using: .utf8)
    mockURLSession = MockURLSession(data: jsonData,
                                    urlResponse: nil,
                                    error: nil)
    sut.session = mockURLSession
    let tokenExpectation = expectation(description: "Token")
    var caughtToken: Token? = nil
    sut.loginUser(withName: "Foo", password: "Bar") { token, _
  in
        caughtToken = token
        tokenExpectation.fulfill()
    }
    waitForExpectations(timeout: 1) { _ in
        XCTAssertEqual(caughtToken?.id, "1234567890")
    }
}
```

First, you set up `sut` with a mock URL session prepared to return a simple JSON. Then, you create an expectation and call the `login` method. The `username` and `password` are irrelevant this time, because you return the simple JSON in the completion handler anyways. At the end of the test, you wait for the expectation to be fulfilled and assert that the token has the expected `id`.

This does not compile because `Token` does not have an `id` property yet. Add the property in the `Token` struct:

```
let id: String
```

Run the test. The test fails because the completion handler in the implementation does nothing right now. Replace the `session.dataTask(with:completionHandler:)` call with the following:

```
session.dataTask(with: url) { (data, response, error) in
    guard let data = data else { return }
    let dict = try! JSONSerialization.jsonObject(
        with: data,
        options: []) as? [String:String]


    let token: Token?
    if let tokenString = dict?["token"] {
        token = Token(id: tokenString)
    } else {
        token = nil
    }
    completion(token, nil)
}.resume()
```

Note that you now call `resume()` on the created data task. Otherwise, the test would not pass because the completion handler would not get called in the test.

This code gets the dictionary from the response data and creates a `Token` instance with the string from the `"token"` key. The created token is then passed to the completion handler of the `login` method.

Run the tests. All the tests pass. There is nothing to refactor even though the code looks bad. Whenever you see an exclamation mark (`!`) in Swift code, you need to figure out whether it is really needed or if the developer (in this case, us) has just been lazy. In the preceding code, you used `try!` to bypass the need for proper error handling. Let's refactor this code using tests to guide the implementation instead.

Handling errors

Using `try!` instead of `try` in the call to `jsonObject(with:options:)`, you tell the compiler: *trust me on this: this method will never fail*. Let's write a test that feeds in wrong data and asserts that an error is thrown:

```
func test_Login_WhenJSONIsInvalid_ReturnsError() {
  mockURLSession = MockURLSession(data: Data(),
                                  urlResponse: nil,
                                  error: nil)

  sut.session = mockURLSession

  let errorExpectation = expectation(description: "Error")
  var catchedError: Error? = nil
  sut.loginUser(withName: "Foo", password: "Bar") { (token, error) in
    catchedError = error
    errorExpectation.fulfill()
  }

  waitForExpectations(timeout: 1) { (error) in
    XCTAssertNotNil(catchedError)
  }
}
```

In the test, you feed an empty data object to the completion handler.

Run the tests. The implementation code crashes because the deserialization fails and throws an error. Change the code so that it handles the thrown error correctly. Replace the content of the completion handler with this:

```
guard let data = data else { return }
do {
  let dict = try JSONSerialization.jsonObject(
    with: data,
    options: []) as? [String:String]

  let token: Token?
  if let tokenString = dict?["token"] {
    token = Token(id: tokenString)
  } else {
    token = nil
  }
  completion(token, nil)
} catch {
  completion(nil, error)
}
```

With this code, you catch the error if there is one, and pass it to the completion block of the login method. Run the tests. All the tests pass again.

Next, you need to make sure that the implementation calls the completion handler with an error when the data value is `nil`. Add the following test:

```
func test_Login_WhenDataIsNil_ReturnsError() {

    mockURLSession = MockURLSession(data: nil,
                                    urlResponse: nil,
                                    error: nil)
    sut.session = mockURLSession

    let errorExpectation = expectation(description: "Error")
    var catchedError: Error? = nil
    sut.loginUser(withName: "Foo", password: "Bar") { (token, error) in
        catchedError = error
        errorExpectation.fulfill()
    }

    waitForExpectations(timeout: 1) { (error) in
        XCTAssertNotNil(catchedError)
    }
}
```

Run the test to make sure it fails.

To make the test pass, you need to define the errors to be thrown. Add the following enum to the end of `APIClient.swift`:

```
enum WebserviceError : Error {
    case DataEmptyError
}
```

Replace the `guard` statement at the beginning of the completion handler in the login method with this:

```
guard let data = data else {
    completion(nil, WebserviceError.DataEmptyError)
    return
}
```

Run the tests. All the tests pass, and there is nothing to refactor.

There is one error left that you need to handle. The completion handler of the data task is called with an `error` parameter. The web service returns any error that has occurred on the server side in this parameter. Our code has to handle this error. Add the following test to make sure that the implementation handles the error when it is set:

```
func test_Login_WhenResponseHasError_ReturnsError() {

    let error = NSError(domain: "SomeError",
                        code: 1234,
                        userInfo: nil)
    let jsonData =
      "{\"token\": \"1234567890\"}"
        .data(using: .utf8)
    mockURLSession = MockURLSession(data: jsonData,
                                urlResponse: nil,
                                error: error)
    sut.session = mockURLSession

    let errorExpectation = expectation(description: "Error")
    var catchedError: Error? = nil
    sut.loginUser(withName: "Foo", password: "Bar") { (token, error) in
        catchedError = error
        errorExpectation.fulfill()
    }

    waitForExpectations(timeout: 1) { (error) in
        XCTAssertNotNil(catchedError)
    }
}
```

Note that you only initialize the mock URL session with valid response data. If you pass in `nil` as data in this test, it would already pass, even though you haven't written the code to handle the response error.

To make this test pass, add the `ResponseError` case to the `WebserviceError` enum, and add the following code to the beginning of the completion handler of the data task:

```
guard error == nil else {
    return completion(nil, error)
}
```

Run the tests. All the tests pass, and there is nothing to refactor.

There are still some tests and implementations for the APIClient class that are missing. You could add tests to fetch an item from and post an item to the web service, for example, to make it possible to access the to-do items from a web application. We won't add the tests in this book because they would look similar to the tests you have already written. But you should add the tests yourself to practice the TDD workflow.

Summary

In this chapter, we wrote tests using test expectations provided by XCTest. We also used stubs to fake a server. We took a look at how both ways bring us closer to our goal--a finished app with as few bugs as possible.

We used dependency injection to catch the completion handler of the session data task in our fake URL session. This way, we could feed test data into the implementation code and assert that the code is implemented as expected. As we controlled the data that the completion handler received, we were able to simulate all kinds of errors and drive the implementation of the correct error handling.

In the following chapter, we will put the different parts of the last few chapters together and finally see the app running.

6
Putting It All Together

In the previous chapters, we implemented different parts of our app using TDD. Now, it is time to put all the parts together to develop a complete app.

This part of the implementation using TDD is the most exciting one. Usually, when not using TDD, you build and run the app in the simulator all the time to check whether your code works and changes bring the app closer to its final state.

In TDD, most of the development is done without running the app on the simulator or device. The tests guide the implementation. This has one big advantage: you can implement parts of the app that need to talk to a component that has not been implemented yet. For example, you can write and verify the complete data model before a view controller or view is able to show the data on the screen.

In this chapter, we will put the different parts of our code together to form the final app. In addition to this, we will take a look at how functional tests can help to find bugs we missed when writing the unit tests.

This chapter covers the following topics:

- Connecting parts
- Serialization and deserialization
- Functional tests

Connecting parts

We will now put the different parts together and implement transitions between them. We need tests for the initial view that is shown after the app is started and for navigating from this view to the other two views. The tests have to ensure that the view controllers have passed the data they need to populate their UIs.

The initial view controller

When you build and run the app now on the simulator, you will only see a black screen. The reason for that is we haven't specified which screen the app should show after it is started. Let's write a test for this. Because this is a test about the storyboard, add **iOS | Source | Unit Test Case Class** to the test target and call it StoryboardTests. Import the main module using the @testable keyword and remove the two template tests.

Add the following test to StoryboardTests:

```
func test_InitialViewController_IsItemListViewController() {
    let storyboard = UIStoryboard(name: "Main", bundle: nil)

    let navigationController =
        storyboard.instantiateInitialViewController()
            as! UINavigationController
    let rootViewController = navigationController.viewControllers[0]

    XCTAssertTrue(rootViewController is ItemListViewController)
}
```

This test gets a reference to the Main storyboard, instantiates its initial view controller (which should be a navigation controller), and gets its root view controller. Then, it asserts that the root view controller is of the type ItemListViewController.

Run the test. The test crashes with an error: unexpectedly found nil while unwrapping an Optional value in the line where we try to initialize the initial view controller. The reason for this is that we have not told Xcode what the initial view controller is.

Open `Main.storyboard`, select the item list view controller and open the Attribute Inspector. Check the checkbox next to **Is Initial View Controller**, as shown in the following screenshot:

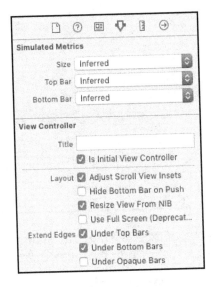

With the item list view controller still selected, navigate to **Editor** | **Embed In** | **Navigation Controller**. With these changes in the storyboard, the initial view controller will be a navigation controller with an instance of `ItemListViewController` as its root view controller.

Run the tests again. All the tests pass and there is nothing to refactor.

Showing the input view

The user should be able to add an item to the list view. As shown in the mockups in `Chapter 2`, *Planning and Structuring Your Test-Driven iOS App*, there should be an **Add** button in the navigation bar that presents the input view controller. We will add the following tests to `ItemListViewControllerTests` because these are tests about `ItemListViewController`.

Open `ItemListViewControllerTests` and add this test:

```
func test_ItemListViewController_HasAddBarButtonWithSelfAsTarget() {
    let target = sut.navigationItem.rightBarButtonItem?.target
    XCTAssertEqual(target as? UIViewController, sut)
}
```

To make this test pass, we need to add a bar button item to the item list view controller. Open `Main.storyboard`, drag a **Bar Button Item** to the navigation bar of the item list view controller, and set the value of **System Item** to **Add**, as shown in the following screenshot:

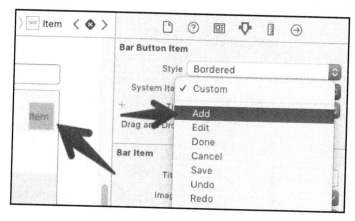

Open `ItemListViewController` in the **Assistant Editor** and *control* + drag from the button to below `viewDidLoad()`, as shown in the following screenshot:

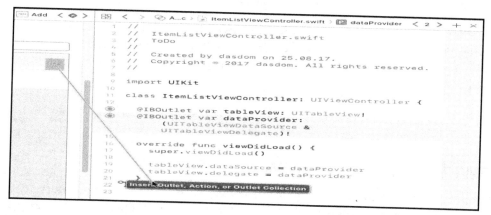

Set the value of **Connection** to `Action`, **Name** to `addItem`, and **Type** to `UIBarButtonItem`.

Run the tests again. The tests pass and there is nothing to refactor.

Next, we want to make sure that the input view controller is presented when the user taps the **Add** button. Add the following test to `ItemListViewControllerTests`:

```
func test_AddItem_PresentsAddItemViewController() {

  XCTAssertNil(sut.presentedViewController)

  guard let addButton = sut.navigationItem.rightBarButtonItem else
  { XCTFail(); return }
  guard let action = addButton.action else { XCTFail(); return }

  sut.performSelector(onMainThread: action,
                      with: addButton,
                      waitUntilDone: true)

  XCTAssertNotNil(sut.presentedViewController)
  XCTAssertTrue(sut.presentedViewController is InputViewController)
}
```

Before we do anything in the test, we make sure that `sut` does not present a view controller on the screen. Then, we get a reference to the **Add** button and perform its selector on `sut`. This makes sense because, from the previous test, we know that `sut` is the target for this button. Run the test to make sure it fails.

To make the test pass, add the following line to the `addItem` method:

```
present(InputViewController(),
        animated: true,
        completion: nil)
```

Run the test. It still fails. To figure out what is going on, navigate to **View | Debug Area | Activate Console**. You should see a line with information similar to this:

```
Warning: Attempt to present <ToDo.InputViewController: 0x7ff2fc75bd90> on
<ToDo.ItemListViewController: 0x7ff2fc75a420> whose view is not in the
window hierarchy!
```

The reason for this warning is that we have just instantiated the view controller, but it is not shown anywhere. It is only possible to present a view controller from another view controller whose view is in the view hierarchy. When the app is running outside of the test, this is not an issue because if the user can tap the **Add** button, the item list view controller must be visible on the screen and therefore its view has to be in the view hierarchy. So, we need to figure out how to write a test for this.

In fact, it is quite easy. We can add the view to the view hierarchy by setting the view controller to the `rootViewController` property of the key window. Add the following line in `test_AddItem_PresentsAddItemViewController()` right below the guard statements:

```
UIApplication.shared.keyWindow?.rootViewController = sut
```

Run the tests again. Now, all the tests pass, but the code looks strange. We instantiate an instance of `InputViewController` using its initializer. This bypasses the storyboard. As a result, the outlet connections we created in Chapter 4, *A Test-Driven View Controller*, are all `nil`. This means that we wouldn't be able to put in the data for the to-do item we want to add.

So, we need another test to make sure that the implementation code instantiates the input view controller instance using the storyboard. Add the following code at the end of `test_AddItem_PresentsAddItemViewController()`:

```
let inputViewController =
  sut.presentedViewController as! InputViewController
XCTAssertNotNil(inputViewController.titleTextField)
```

Run the test to make sure it is red. To make the test pass, replace the contents of `addItem(_:)` with the following code:

```
@IBAction func addItem(_ sender: AnyObject) {
  if let nextViewController =
    storyboard?.instantiateViewController(
      withIdentifier: "InputViewController")
      as? InputViewController {

    present(nextViewController, animated: true, completion: nil)
  }
}
```

This code instantiates an instance of `InputViewController` from the storyboard and presents it on the screen. Run the tests. All the tests pass.

To be able to add items to the list, `ItemListViewController` and `InputViewController` need to share the same item manager. This is possible because `ItemManager` is a class and therefore both view controllers can hold a reference to the same instance. If we had used `struct` instead, adding an item in `InputViewController` would not have changed the item manager referenced by `ItemListViewController`.

Let's write a test to make sure that both view controllers refer to the same object. Add the following test to `ItemListViewControllerTests`:

```
func testItemListVC_SharesItemManagerWithInputVC() {

    guard let addButton = sut.navigationItem.rightBarButtonItem else
    { XCTFail(); return }
    guard let action = addButton.action else { XCTFail(); return }
    UIApplication.shared.keyWindow?.rootViewController = sut

    sut.performSelector(onMainThread: action,
                        with: addButton,
                        waitUntilDone: true)

    guard let inputViewController =
        sut.presentedViewController as? InputViewController else
    { XCTFail(); return }
    guard let inputItemManager = inputViewController.itemManager else
    { XCTFail(); return }
    XCTAssertTrue(sut.itemManager === inputItemManager)
}
```

The first part of the test is similar to the earlier test. After presenting the input view controller on the screen, we assert that `itemManager` in `inputViewControler` refers to the same object as `sut`.

This test does not compile because `Value of type 'ItemListViewController' has no member 'itemManger'`. Add the following property to make it compile:

```
let itemManager = ItemManager()
```

Run the test. It compiles but fails because `itemManager` of `inputViewController` is nil. Add the following line in `addItem(_:)` right before the next view controller is presented:

```
nextViewController.itemManager = ItemManager()
```

Run the test. It still fails, but this time it's because the item manager of `sut` and input view controller do not refer to the same object. Replace the line you just added with this one:

```
nextViewController.itemManager = itemManager
```

Run all the tests. All the tests pass.

If you look at the last two tests, there is a lot of duplicated code. The tests need refactoring. This is left as an exercise for you. You should be able to extract the duplicated code with the knowledge you have gained so far.

Now, let's check whether we can add a to-do item to the list. Build and run the app. Tap the plus (+) button and put a title into the text field connected to the `titleTextField` property. Tap the **Save** button (the one that is connected to the `save` action). Nothing happens. The reason for this is that we did not add the code to dismiss the view controller when the **Save** button was tapped. We need a test for this.

Open `InputViewControllerTests.swift` and add the following definition of a mock class after the other mock classes:

```
class MockInputViewController : InputViewController {

    var dismissGotCalled = false

    override func dismiss(animated flag: Bool,
                          completion: (() -> Void)? = nil) {

        dismissGotCalled = true
    }
}
```

The mock class is a subclass of `InputViewController`. The correct term for such a mock is partial mock because it only mocks parts of the behavior of its super class. With this in place, we can write the test:

```
func testSave_DismissesViewController() {
    let mockInputViewController = MockInputViewController()
    mockInputViewController.titleTextField = UITextField()
    mockInputViewController.dateTextField = UITextField()
    mockInputViewController.locationTextField = UITextField()
    mockInputViewController.addressTextField = UITextField()
    mockInputViewController.descriptionTextField = UITextField()
    mockInputViewController.titleTextField.text = "Test Title"

    mockInputViewController.save()

    XCTAssertTrue(mockInputViewController.dismissGotCalled)
}
```

As we do not instantiate from the storyboard, we need to set the text fields in the test; otherwise, the test will crash because it will try to access text fields that are `nil`. After this, we set a test `title` to the `title` text field and call `save`. This should dismiss the view controller.

Run the test. It fails. To make it pass is quite easy. Add the following line at the end of save():

```
dismiss(animated: true)
```

Now, run all the tests. All the tests pass.

Let's take a look at what the app looks like now. Build and run the app in the simulator, tap the **Add** button, put in a title, and hit **Save**. The input view controller is dismissed but no item is added to the list. There are two problems concerning this micro feature. First, the item manager defined in ItemListViewController is not shared with the data provider. Second, after an item has been added to the list, we need to tell the table view to reload its data.

Let's write a test for the first problem. Add the following test to ItemListViewController:

```
func test_ViewDidLoad_SetsItemManagerToDataProvider() {
    XCTAssertTrue(sut.itemManager === sut.dataProvider.itemManager)
}
```

This test does not compile because the data provider is of the type (UITableViewDataSource & UITableViewDelegate)!. The compiler cannot know that it also has an itemManager property. To fix this, add the following protocol to ItemDataProvider.swift outside of the class definition:

```
@objc protocol ItemManagerSettable {
    var itemManager: ItemManager? { get set }
}
```

Now, the static analyzer tells us that this property cannot be a member of an @objc protocol because its type cannot be represented in Objective-C. But, we need to declare the protocol to be @objc because we've set the data provider from the storyboard. The solution is to make ItemManager a subclass of NSObject:

```
class ItemManager: NSObject {
    // ....
}
```

Now, we can make `ItemListDataProvider` conform to `ItemManagerSettable` as follows:

```
class ItemListDataProvider: NSObject, UITableViewDataSource,
UITableViewDelegate, ItemManagerSettable {
    // ....
}
```

We can finally add the protocol in the declaration of the data provider in `ItemListViewController`:

```
@IBOutlet var dataProvider: (UITableViewDataSource & UITableViewDelegate &
ItemManagerSettable)!
```

Run the test. Finally, the test compiles but it fails. To make it pass, add the following line at the end of `viewDidLoad()` in `ItemListViewController`:

```
dataProvider.itemManager = itemManager
```

Now, run all the tests. All the tests pass again and there is nothing to refactor.

On to the next problem: we need to make sure that the table view is reloaded when an item is added to the item manager. A perfect place for the reload is `viewWillAppear(_:)`. As an exercise, add this test to `ItemListViewControllerTests`. You may need a mock for the table view to register when `reloadData()` is called. A reminder: to trigger `viewWillAppear(_:)`, do this in your test:

```
sut.beginAppearanceTransition(true, animated: true)
sut.endAppearanceTransition()
```

Write the test as an exercise.

To make the test pass, add the following code to `ItemListViewController`:

```
override func viewWillAppear(_ animated: Bool) {
    super.viewWillAppear(animated)

    tableView.reloadData()
}
```

Finally, build and run the app again and add an item to the list. You should see something like this:

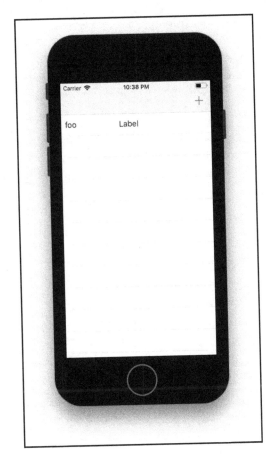

If adding a to-do item doesn't work when you run the app, make sure that you have implemented the `else` path in `add()` no location is added to the location text field. It should look like this:

```
let item = ToDoItem(title: titleString,
                    itemDescription: descriptionString,
                    timestamp: date?.timeIntervalSince1970,
                    location: nil)
self.itemManager?.add(item)
```

Showing the detail view

When the user taps a cell, the detail view should be shown on the screen with the information of the corresponding to-do item. The selection of the cell is managed by the data provider because it is the delegate for the table view. The presentation of the detail view controller is managed by the item list view controller. This means the data provider has to communicate the selection of a cell to the list view controller. There are several different ways to achieve this. We will use a notification because it will be interesting to take a look at how we can test sending of notifications.

Communication with notifications has two partners: the sender and the receiver. In our case, the sender is the data provider. Let's write a test that ensures that a notification is sent when the user selects a cell. Open `ItemListDataProviderTests` and add the following test method:

```
func test_SelectingACell_SendsNotification() {
    let item = ToDoItem(title: "First")
    sut.itemManager?.add(item)

    expectation(
      forNotification: NSNotification.Name(
        rawValue: "ItemSelectedNotification"),
      object: nil) { (notification) -> Bool in

        guard let index =
          notification.userInfo?["index"] as? Int else
        { return false }

        return index == 0
    }

    tableView.delegate?.tableView!(
      tableView,
      didSelectRowAt: IndexPath(row: 0, section: 0))

    waitForExpectations(timeout: 3, handler: nil)
}
```

First, we add an item to the item manager to create a cell that we can select. Then, we create an expectation for a notification. When a notification with that name is sent, the closure is called. In the closure, we check whether the user information contains an index and the index is equal to 0. If it is, the closure will return `true`; otherwise, it'll return `false`. A return value of `true` means that the expectation is fulfilled. Next, we will call `didSelectRowAt` on the table view's delegate and wait for the expectation to be fulfilled.

Run the test. It fails. To make the test pass, add the following code to
`ItemListDataProvider`:

```
func tableView(_ tableView: UITableView,
                didSelectRowAt indexPath: IndexPath) {
  guard let itemSection = Section(rawValue: indexPath.section) else
  { fatalError() }

  switch itemSection {
  case .toDo:
    NotificationCenter.default.post(
        name: NSNotification.Name("ItemSelectedNotification"),
        object: self,
        userInfo: ["index": indexPath.row])

  default:
    break
  }
}
```

This code is straightforward. We get the section, and if the tap is in the to-do section, we
send the notification with the tapped row in `userInfo`.

Run all the tests. All the tests pass and there is nothing to refactor.

The receiver of the notification should be the item list view controller, and it'll push the
detail view controller onto the navigation stack when it receives the message. To test this,
we need another mock. Add the following code in
`ItemListViewControllerTests.swift` but outside of the
class `ItemListViewControllerTests`:

```
extension ItemListViewControllerTests {
  class MockNavigationController : UINavigationController {

    var lastPushedViewController: UIViewController?

    override func pushViewController(_ viewController:
                                    UIViewController,
                                    animated: Bool)

    {
      lastPushedViewController = viewController
      super.pushViewController(viewController, animated: animated)
    }
  }
}
```

This is a mock for `UINavigationController`, and it simply registers when a view controller is pushed onto the navigation stack.

Add the following test to `ItemListViewControllerTests`:

```
func testItemSelectedNotification_PushesDetailVC() {

    let mockNavigationController =
    MockNavigationController(rootViewController: sut)

    UIApplication.shared.keyWindow?.rootViewController =
    mockNavigationController

    sut.loadViewIfNeeded()
    sut.itemManager.add(ToDoItem(title: "foo"))
    sut.itemManager.add(ToDoItem(title: "bar"))
    NotificationCenter.default.post(
      name: NSNotification.Name("ItemSelectedNotification"),
      object: self,
      userInfo: ["index": 1])

    guard let detailViewController = mockNavigationController
      .lastPushedViewController as? DetailViewController else {
        return XCTFail()
    }

    guard let detailItemManager = detailViewController.itemInfo?.0 else
    { return XCTFail() }

    guard let index = detailViewController.itemInfo?.1 else
    { return XCTFail() }

    detailViewController.loadViewIfNeeded()

    XCTAssertNotNil(detailViewController.titleLabel)
    XCTAssertTrue(detailItemManager === sut.itemManager)
    XCTAssertEqual(index, 1)
}
```

There are many lines of code. Let's go through them step by step. First, we create an instance of our navigation controller mock and set its root view controller to be the `sut` property. As seen earlier, in order to be able to push a view controller onto the navigation stack, the view of the pushing view controller has to be in the view hierarchy. Then, we load the view of `sut` to trigger `viewDidLoad()` because we assume that `sut` is added as an observer to `NotificationCenter.default` in `viewDidLoad()`. With this setup, we can send the notification using `NotificationCenter.default`. Next, we get the pushed view controller and assert that it is of the `DetailViewController` type. Then, we check whether the item's information is passed to the pushed view controller. Finally, we check whether `titleLabel` of the detail view controller is not nil and if it shares the item manager with the item list view controller.

Run the test. The test fails. To make the test pass, we first need to add `ItemListViewController` as an observer to `NotificationCenter.default`. Add the following code at the end of `viewDidLoad()`:

```
NotificationCenter.default.addObserver(
    self,
    selector: #selector(showDetails(sender:)),
    name: NSNotification.Name("ItemSelectedNotification"),
    object: nil)
```

Next, we have to implement `showDetails(_:)`. Add the following method to `ItemListViewController`:

```
@objc func showDetails(sender: NSNotification) {
    guard let index = sender.userInfo?["index"] as? Int else
    { fatalError() }

    if let nextViewController = storyboard?.instantiateViewController(
        withIdentifier: "DetailViewController") as? DetailViewController {

        nextViewController.itemInfo = (itemManager, index)
        navigationController?.pushViewController(nextViewController,
                                                 animated: true)

    }
}
```

Run all the tests. All the tests pass and there is nothing to refactor.

Serialization and deserialization

You may notice that the to-do item you put in is gone when you restart the app. Such an app is useless for the user. The app needs to store the to-do items somehow and reload them when it is opened the next time. There are different possibilities to implement this. We could use Core Data, serialize the data using `NSCoding`, or use a third-party framework. In this book, we will write the date into a **property list (plist)**. A plist has the advantage that it can be opened and altered with Xcode or any other editor.

The data model we implemented uses structs. Unfortunately, structs cannot be written to a plist. We have to convert the data into `Any` arrays and `String:Any` dictionaries. Add the following code to `ToDoItemTests`:

```
func test_HasPlistDictionaryProperty() {
    let item = ToDoItem(title: "First")
    let dictionary = item.plistDict
}
```

The static analyzer complains that there is no property with the name `plistDict`. Let's add it. Open `ToDoItem` and add the property:

```
var plistDict: String {
    return ""
}
```

We will use a calculated property here because we don't want to initialize it during initialization, and the value should be calculated from the current values of the other properties. Add the following assertions at the end of the test:

```
XCTAssertNotNil(dictionary)
XCTAssertTrue(dictionary is [String:Any])
```

As mentioned previously, to be able to write the date into a plist, it needs to be of type `[String:Any]`. Run the test. It fails because, right now, the calculated property is of type `String`. Replace the property with this code:

```
var plistDict: [String:Any] {
    return [:]
}
```

Run all the tests. All the tests pass and there is nothing to refactor.

Now, we need to make sure that we can recreate an item from `plistDict`. Add the following code to `ToDoItemTests`:

```
func test_CanBeCreatedFromPlistDictionary() {
    let location = Location(name: "Bar")
    let item = ToDoItem(title: "Foo",
                        itemDescription: "Baz",
                        timestamp: 1.0,
                        location: location)

    let dict = item.plistDict
    let recreatedItem = ToDoItem(dict: dict)
}
```

We have to stop writing the test because the static analyzer complains `The 'ToDoItem' struct does not have an initializer with a parameter named 'dict'`. Open `ToDoItem.swift` and add the following code to the `ToDoItem` struct:

```
init?(dict: [String:Any]) {
    return nil
}
```

This is enough to make the test compilable. Now, add the assertion to the test:

```
XCTAssertEqual(item, recreatedItem)
```

That assertion asserts that the recreated item is the same as the item used to create `plistDict`. Run the test. The test fails because we haven't implemented writing the data of struct to `[String:Any]` and the creation of a to-do item from `[String:Any]`. To write the complete information needed to recreate a to-do item into a dictionary, we first have to make sure that an instance of `Location` can be written to and recreated from `[String:Any]`.

In TDD, it is important to always have only one failing test. So, before we can move to the tests for `Location`, we have to disable the last test we wrote. During test execution, the test runner searches for methods in the test cases that begin with test. Change the name of the previous test method to `xtest_CanBeCreatedFromPlistDictionary()`. Run the tests to make sure that all tests, except this one, are executed.

Now, open `LocationTests` and add the following code:

```
func test_CanBeSerializedAndDeserialized() {
    let location = Location(
        name: "Home",
        coordinate: CLLocationCoordinate2DMake(50.0, 6.0))

    let dict = location.plistDict
}
```

Again, the static analyzer complains because the property is missing. We already know how to make this compilable again. Add this code to `Location`:

```
var plistDict: [String:Any] {
    return [:]
}
```

With this change, the test compiles. Add the following code to the end of the test:

```
XCTAssertNotNil(dict)
let recreatedLocation = Location(dict: dict)
```

Again, this does not compile because `Location` does not have an initializer with one parameter called `dict`. Let's add it:

```
init?(dict: [String:Any]) {
    return nil
}
```

The test passes again. But it is not finished yet. We need to make sure that the recreated location is the same as the one we used to create the `[String:Any]`. Add the assertion at the end of the test:

```
XCTAssertEqual(location, recreatedLocation)
```

Run the test. It fails. To make it pass, the `plistDict` property has to have all the information needed to recreate the location. Replace the calculated property with this code:

```
private let nameKey = "nameKey"
private let latitudeKey = "latitudeKey"
private let longitudeKey = "longitudeKey"


var plistDict: [String:Any] {
    var dict = [String:Any]()

    dict[nameKey] = name
```

```
  if let coordinate = coordinate {
    dict[latitudeKey] = coordinate.latitude
    dict[longitudeKey] = coordinate.longitude
  }
  return dict
}
```

The code explains itself. It just puts all the information of a location into an instance of [String:Any]. Now, replace the initializer with the dict argument with the following:

```
init?(dict: [String:Any]) {
  guard let name = dict[nameKey] as? String else
  { return nil }

  let coordinate: CLLocationCoordinate2D?
  if let latitude = dict[latitudeKey] as? Double,
    let longitude = dict[longitudeKey] as? Double {
    coordinate = CLLocationCoordinate2DMake(latitude, longitude)
  } else {
    coordinate = nil
  }

  self.name = name
  self.coordinate = coordinate
}
```

Run the tests. All the tests pass again.

As the location can be written to [String:Any], we can use it for the serialization of ToDoItem. Open ToDoItemTests again, and remove the x at the beginning of the method name of xtest_CanBeCreatedFromPlistDictionary(). Run the tests to make sure that this test fails.

Now, replace the implementation of the calculated plistDict property in ToDoItem with this code:

```
private let titleKey = "titleKey"
private let itemDescriptionKey = "itemDescriptionKey"
private let timestampKey = "timestampKey"
private let locationKey = "locationKey"

var plistDict: [String:Any] {
  var dict = [String:Any]()
  dict[titleKey] = title
  if let itemDescription = itemDescription {
    dict[itemDescriptionKey] = itemDescription
  }
```

```
if let timestamp = timestamp {
    dict[timestampKey] = timestamp
}
if let location = location {
    let locationDict = location.plistDict
    dict[locationKey] = locationDict
}
return dict
}
```

Again, this is straightforward. We will put all the values stored in the properties into a dictionary and return it. To recreate a to-do item from a `plist` dictionary, replace `init?(dict:)` with this:

```
init?(dict: [String:Any]) {
    guard let title = dict[titleKey] as? String else
    { return nil }

    self.title = title

    self.itemDescription = dict[itemDescriptionKey] as? String
    self.timestamp = dict[timestampKey] as? Double
    if let locationDict = dict[locationKey] as? [String:Any] {
        self.location = Location(dict: locationDict)
    } else {
        self.location = nil
    }
}
```

In this `init` method, we fill the properties of `ToDoItem` with the values from the dictionary. Run the tests. All the tests pass and there is nothing to refactor.

The next step is to write the list of checked and unchecked to-do items to the disk and restore them when the app is started again. To drive the implementation, we will write a test that creates two to-do items and adds them to an item manager, sets the item manager to `nil`, and then, creates a new one. The created item manager should then have the same items as the one that got destroyed. Open `ItemManagerTests` and add the following test in it:

```
func test_ToDoItemsGetSerialized() {
    var itemManager: ItemManager? = ItemManager()

    let firstItem = ToDoItem(title: "First")
    itemManager!.add(firstItem)

    let secondItem = ToDoItem(title: "Second")
    itemManager!.add(secondItem)
```

```
NotificationCenter.default.post(
    name: .UIApplicationWillResignActive,
    object: nil)

itemManager = nil

XCTAssertNil(itemManager)

itemManager = ItemManager()
XCTAssertEqual(itemManager?.toDoCount, 2)
XCTAssertEqual(itemManager?.item(at: 0), firstItem)
XCTAssertEqual(itemManager?.item(at: 1), secondItem)
}
```

In this test, we first create an item manager, add two to-do items, and send `UIApplicationWillResignActive` to signal to the app that it should write the data to disk. Next, we set the item manager to `nil` to destroy it. Then, we create a new item manager and assert that it has the same items.

Run the test. The test crashes because we try to access a to-do item in the item manager but there is no item yet.

Before we write the code that writes the to-do items to disk, add the following code to `tearDown()`, right before `super.tearDown()`:

```
sut.removeAllItems()
sut = nil
```

This is needed because, otherwise, all the tests would end up writing their to-do items to disk, and the tests would not start from a clean state.

As mentioned previously, the item manager should register as an observer for `UIApplicationWillResignActive` and write the data to disk when the notification is sent. Add the following `init` method to `ItemManager`:

```
override init() {
    super.init()

    NotificationCenter.default.addObserver(
        self,
        selector: #selector(save),
        name: .UIApplicationWillResignActive,
        object: nil)
}
```

The enum with the value `UIApplicationWillResignActive` is defined in `UIKit`, so replace `import Foundation` with `import UIKit`. Next, add the following calculated property to create a path URL for the plist:

```
var toDoPathURL: URL {
    let fileURLs = FileManager.default.urls(
        for: .documentDirectory, in: .userDomainMask)

    guard let documentURL = fileURLs.first else {
        print("Something went wrong. Documents url could not be found")
        fatalError()
    }

    return documentURL.appendingPathComponent("toDoItems.plist")
}
```

This code gets the `document` directory of the app and appends the `toDoItems.plist` path component. Now, we can write the `save` method:

```
@objc func save() {
    let nsToDoItems = toDoItems.map { $0.plistDict }

    guard nsToDoItems.count > 0 else {
        try? FileManager.default.removeItem(at: toDoPathURL)
        return
    }
    do {
        let plistData = try PropertyListSerialization.data(
            fromPropertyList: nsToDoItems,
            format: PropertyListSerialization.PropertyListFormat.xml,
            options: PropertyListSerialization.WriteOptions(0)
        )
        try plistData.write(to: toDoPathURL,
                        options: Data.WritingOptions.atomic)
    } catch {
        print(error)
    }
}
```

First, we create an `Any` array with the dictionaries of the to-do items. If the array has at least one item, we write it to the disk using the `PropertyListSerialization` class. Otherwise, we remove whatever is stored at the location of the file path.

When a new item manager is created, we have to read the data from the plist and fill the `toDoItems` array. The perfect place to read the data is in the `init` method. Add the following code at the end of `init()`:

```
if let nsToDoItems = NSArray(contentsOf: toDoPathURL) {

    for dict in nsToDoItems {
        if let toDoItem = ToDoItem(dict: dict as! [String:Any]) {
            toDoItems.append(toDoItem)
        }
    }
}
```

Before we can run the tests, we need to do some housekeeping. We have added the item manager as an observer to `NotificationCenter.default`. Like good citizens, we have to remove it when we aren't interested in notifications anymore. Add the following `deinit` method to `ItemManager`:

```
deinit {
    NotificationCenter.default.removeObserver(self)
    save()
}
```

In addition to removing the observer, we call `save()` to trigger the save operation.

There are many lines of code needed to make one test pass. We could have broken these down into smaller steps. In fact, you should experiment with the test and the implementation and see what happens when you comment out parts of it.

Run all tests. Uh!? A lot of unrelated tests fail.

If you do not see failing tests, the timing of your tests might be different to mine. Do the following changes anyway because, otherwise, you might see failing tests later.

We haven't changed the code the other tests are testing, but we changed the way `ItemManager` works. If you have a look at `ItemListDataProviderTests`, `DetailViewControllerTests`, and `InputViewControllerTests`, we added items to an item manager instance in there. This means that we need to clean up after the tests have been executed. Open `ItemListDataProviderTests` and add the following code to `tearDown()`, right before `super.tearDown()`:

```
sut.itemManager?.removeAll()
```

Add the same code to `tearDown()` in `InputViewControllerTests`.

Now, add the following to `tearDown()` in `DetailViewControllerTests`:

```
sut.itemInfo?.0.removeAll()
```

Run the tests again. All the tests pass. We will move to the next section, but you should implement the tests and code for the serialization and deserialization of the done items in `ItemManager`.

Functional tests

Until now, we have written unit tests to drive the implementation. Unit tests test a small microfeature (a unit of the project) under controlled circumstances.

On the other side of the spectrum are functional tests, which test the functionalities of the app in terms of how a user would approach them. The user does not care how the app they're using is implemented. The user cares about what they can do with the app. Functional tests help make sure that the app works as expected.

In this section, we will add a functional test using UI tests, which were introduced with Xcode 7. We will take one functionality (adding a to-do item) and write a test from the user's perspective.

Adding a UI test target

First, we need to add a UI test target to our project. In Project Navigator, select the project and click on the button at the bottom of the view showing the target list:

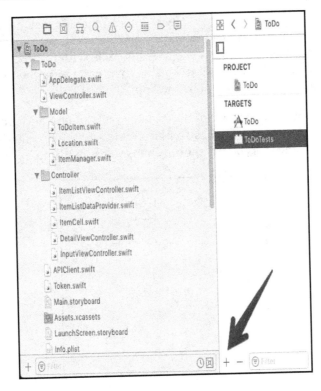

From the template chooser, navigate to **iOS | Test | iOS UI Testing Bundle**. Let the name remain as Xcode suggests it, click on **Next**, and then on **Finish**.

Recording and testing

Open Project Navigator and scroll down to the `ToDoUITests` group. In the group, you'll find a file called `ToDoUITests.swift`. Click on it to open it in the editor. The structure of the file is similar to the other test cases. In fact, the UI test class is a subclass of `XCTextCase`, like all our other test cases. Take a look at `setUp()`. You'll see this line:

```
XCUIApplication().launch()
```

This line launches the app for the UI test. Here, you can already see the difference between unit tests and UI tests. A unit test just loads the classes it needs for the test. It doesn't matter how the classes are put together or how the user interacts with the app. In UI tests, the test runner needs to launch the app in order to be able to interact with the real UI. The user interacts with the same UI when they start the app.

Before we write the functional test, open `Main.storyboard` and add **Auto Layout** constraints to position the views. Then, add placeholders to the text fields of the input view controller. The scene in the storyboard should then look something like this:

Also, add constraints to the other views in the storyboard.

Now, go back to `ToDoUITests`, remove the comment, and position the cursor within the method `testExample`. At the bottom of the editor, you'll see a red dot:

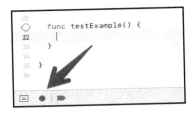

Click on it to start recording the UI test. Xcode compiles the app and launches it in the simulator. When the app is running, click on the **Add** button to navigate to the input screen. Then, put in the values for all the fields and click on **Save**. Remember to put the date in the `02/22/2016` format because this is the format we used when we built `InputViewController`.

While you were interacting with the UI, Xcode recorded your actions. Open `ToDoUITests` and have a look at the code. The recording doesn't always produce the same code but, in general, it should look like this (if the recording didn't work, just copy and paste the code into the `test` method):

```
let app = XCUIApplication()
app.navigationBars["ToDo.ItemListView"].buttons["Add"].tap()

let titleTextField = app.textFields["Title"]
titleTextField.tap()
titleTextField.typeText("Meeting")

let dateTextField = app.textFields["Date"]
dateTextField.tap()
dateTextField.typeText("02/22/2018")

let locationNameTextField = app.textFields["Location"]
locationNameTextField.tap()
locationNameTextField.typeText("Office")

let addressTextField = app.textFields["Address"]
addressTextField.tap()
addressTextField.typeText("Infinite Loop 1, Cupertino")

let descriptionTextField = app.textFields["Description"]
descriptionTextField.tap()
descriptionTextField.typeText("Bring iPad")
app.buttons["Save"].tap()
```

Let's take a look at what happens when we run the test. Click on the diamond next to the beginning of the `test` method and switch to the simulator. Like magic, Xcode will run your app and interact with the UI.

But there is something strange. After the test runner has tapped **Save**, the input screen is dismissed and the list view is shown. But, where is the item? It is not added to the list. It looks like we have a bug in our code.

Let's add assertions to the test to make sure we fix this bug. Add the following code at the end of the test:

```
XCTAssertTrue(app.tables.staticTexts["Meeting"].exists)
XCTAssertTrue(app.tables.staticTexts["02/22/2018"].exists)
XCTAssertTrue(app.tables.staticTexts["Office"].exists)
```

Run the UI test to make sure it fails.

Now, open `InputViewController` and let's see if we can spot the problem. If you would like to find the bug yourself, add breakpoints and step through the code (and stop reading further until you have found it).

Did you find it? As described earlier, the geocoder is asynchronous. This means that the call back closure is executed on a different thread. The main thread does not wait until the geocoder has finished its work and dismisses the view controller before an item can be added to the item manager.

Let's fix this bug. First, remove the following line of code:

```
dismiss(animated: true)
```

Next, change the code according to the following code:

```
// ...

if let locationName = locationTextField.text,
  locationName.characters.count > 0 {
  if let address = addressTextField.text,
    address.characters.count > 0 {

    geocoder.geocodeAddressString(address) {
      [unowned self] (placeMarks, error) -> Void in

      let placeMark = placeMarks?.first

      let item = ToDoItem(
        title: titleString,
        itemDescription: descriptionString,
```

```
          timestamp: date?.timeIntervalSince1970,
          location: Location(
            name: locationName,
            coordinate: placeMark?.location?.coordinate))

        DispatchQueue.main.async(execute: {
          self.itemManager?.add(item)
          self.dismiss(animated: true)
        })
      }
    } else {
      let item = ToDoItem(title: titleString,
                          itemDescription: descriptionString,
                          timestamp: date?.timeIntervalSince1970,
                          location: nil)
      self.itemManager?.add(item)
      dismiss(animated: true)
    }
  } else {
    let item = ToDoItem(title: titleString,
                        itemDescription: descriptionString,
                        timestamp: date?.timeIntervalSince1970,
                        location: nil)
    self.itemManager?.add(item)
    dismiss(animated: true)
  }
}
```

Run the test. Now, the test passes. We have just recorded and written our first functional test. You should add the missing functional tests, for example, in order to check and uncheck items and show their details.

To make sure we haven't broken anything due to these changes, let's run all the tests again. Bummer. The test execution crashes in `test_Save_UsesGeocoderToGetCoordinateFromAddress()` when we try to access the item at index 0. The reason for this crash is that we call `add(_:)` in the `save()` method on a different thread. This means that the assertions are executed before the item is added to the item manager. We need to make the test asynchronous to account for the change in the implementation.

Open `InputViewControllerTests` and replace `MockInputViewController` with this code:

```
class MockInputViewController : InputViewController {

  var dismissGotCalled = false
  var completionHandler: (() -> Void)?

  override func dismiss(animated flag: Bool,
                        completion: (() -> Void)? = nil) {

    dismissGotCalled = true
    completionHandler?()
  }
}
```

By making this change, we added the ability to get notified when `dismiss` (`animated:completion:`) is called. We need to change the test to use the input view controller mock and add code to make the test asynchronous. Replace `test_Save_UsesGeocoderToGetCoordinateFromAddress()` with the following code:

```
func test_Save_UsesGeocoderToGetCoordinateFromAddress() {
  let mockSut = MockInputViewController()

  mockSut.titleTextField = UITextField()
  mockSut.dateTextField = UITextField()
  mockSut.locationTextField = UITextField()
  mockSut.addressTextField = UITextField()
  mockSut.descriptionTextField = UITextField()

  let dateFormatter = DateFormatter()
  dateFormatter.dateFormat = "MM/dd/yyyy"

  let timestamp = 1456095600.0
  let date = Date(timeIntervalSince1970: timestamp)


  mockSut.titleTextField.text = "Foo"
  mockSut.dateTextField.text = dateFormatter.string(from: date)
  mockSut.locationTextField.text = "Bar"
  mockSut.addressTextField.text = "Infinite Loop 1, Cupertino"
  mockSut.descriptionTextField.text = "Baz"
  let mockGeocoder = MockGeocoder()
  mockSut.geocoder = mockGeocoder

  mockSut.itemManager = ItemManager()
```

```
let dismissExpectation = expectation(description: "Dismiss")

mockSut.completionHandler = {
  dismissExpectation.fulfill()
}

mockSut.save()

placemark = MockPlacemark()
let coordinate = CLLocationCoordinate2DMake(37.3316851,
                                            -122.0300674)

placemark.mockCoordinate = coordinate
mockGeocoder.completionHandler?([placemark], nil)

waitForExpectations(timeout: 1, handler: nil)

let item = mockSut.itemManager?.item(at: 0)

let testItem = ToDoItem(title: "Foo",
                itemDescription: "Baz",
                timestamp: timestamp,
                location: Location(name: "Bar",
                                   coordinate: coordinate))

XCTAssertEqual(item, testItem)
mockSut.itemManager?.removeAll()
}
```

This looks more complicated than it is. We just replaced `sut` with an instance of `MockInputViewController`. As seen earlier, because we are not using the storyboard, we need to set the text fields. We need to remove all items from the item manager, otherwise, the added item would get serialized.

Run all the tests. Now, all the tests pass.

Summary

In this chapter, you took a look at how tests guide you toward the final steps to create the complete app. You used tests to drive the implementation of the navigation between the view controllers of the app. You also implemented the serialization and deserialization of the to-do items.

Finally, you used functional tests to make sure that the app worked from the user perspective, and you found a critical bug by doing so.

In the next chapter, you will take a look at the code coverage of your tests. This means that you will get a better insight into how much of the code is covered by tests. You will also set up continuous integration in order to improve the feedback about your code.

7
Code Coverage

We now have about 80 tests and the code that makes tests pass, but do the tests really test all the code? Using TDD, the code coverage of our tests should be quite high. *Should.*

Instead of guessing, we would rather have numbers that tell us how good the code coverage of our tests really is. Before Xcode 7, it was quite difficult to measure the coverage of a test suite, but with version 7, Apple added this feature to Xcode.

In this chapter, we will measure the code coverage of our tests, and we will take a look at how we can use Xcode Server and fastlane to automate everyday tasks in our lives as iOS developers. The chapter is structured like this:

- Enabling code coverage
- Automatic deployment with fastlane

Enabling code coverage

Measuring the code coverage of our tests gives us a feeling of completeness about our test suite. While following the TDD workflow, as we don't write any code without a failing test, the code coverage of our project should be very high. We don't expect it to be 100%, meaning that all the code paths are executed in the tests because the static analyzer forces us to write code that we don't expect to be executed. For example, in the code we wrote, we often used `guard` to make sure that the value we wanted to access was not nil. We could have written tests for a case where the value was `nil`. But in my opinion, in most cases these tests give no additional value.

Nevertheless, we will examine the parts of the project without code coverage and discuss whether we need to add tests to cover them.

Code coverage in Xcode

Xcode has added native support for the measurement of the code coverage of tests with version 7. To enable it, select **Edit Scheme...** in the scheme selector in Xcode:

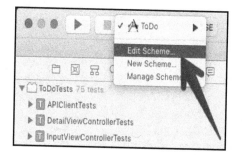

In the following pop-up window, select the **Test** phase and check **Gather coverage data**:

That is all! If you have tried to add the gathering of code coverage in Xcode 6, you will most probably be impressed by how easy this is in Xcode 9. Close the window, and run all the tests to measure the code coverage.

After the tests have finished, select the Report Navigator, click on **Test**, and select the **Coverage** tab, as shown in the following screenshot:

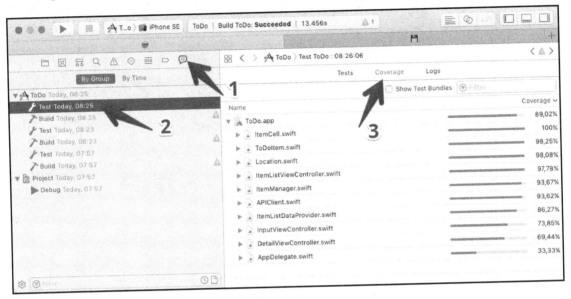

This opens the **Coverage** data view. On the left-hand side, you can see the files in the project, and on the right-hand side, the corresponding coverage value is shown. The worst coverage is in `AppDelegate.swift`. Click on the triangle next to the filename to expand its details. The details show the coverage data for all the methods in the file. It immediately becomes clear why the code coverage in `AppDelegate.swift` is that low. We left the methods from the template in `AppDelegate` even though we don't need them.

Let's remove the unused methods. Open `AppDelegate.swift`. The only really required method here is `application(_:didFinishLaunchingWithOptions:)`. Remove all the other methods, run all the tests, and open the code coverage for the new test run. Now, `AppDelegate` has 100% test coverage. Great!

Let's take a look at another file where the code coverage is not 100%. Open
`DetailViewController.swift` and go to **Editor | Show Code Coverage**. If you cannot
find the menu item and, instead, there is an item called **Hide Code Coverage**, it means that
your editor is already set up correctly. With this setting, Xcode shows the coverage data in
the editor next to the code:

The numbers show how often this code block has been executed during the test's run. If the
number is **0**, it means that this line did not get executed. This is strange. Why isn't the code
in the date formatter executed? I think this is a bug. Apple rewrote the code editor in Xcode
9. A rewrite of something as complex as the editor in Xcode is not simple. This means, take
the code coverage info in the editor with a grain of salt.

In the case of `DetailViewController.swift`, the following line has no code coverage:

```
guard let itemInfo = itemInfo else { return }
```

To take a look at what is going on here, let's replace this line with the following equivalent implementation:

```
guard let itemInfo = itemInfo
  else { return }
```

Run the tests again to collect the coverage data. The code coverage is zero in the line with the `else` clause. The reason for this is that we did not write a test for the case when `itemInfo` was `nil`. Do we need this test? In my opinion, in this case, it does not make sense to add a test for this because we will just return from `viewWillAppear(_:)` when `itemInfo` is `nil`. In addition to this, in our app, the only controller that creates an instance of `DetailViewController` is `ItemListViewController`, and we already have a test that this controller sets in the `itemInfo` dictionary.

In fact, it is a development error if we forget to set `itemInfo` because then the detail view controller will not be able to show any useful data. So, instead of adding a test, we'd rather make sure that the app crashes when there isn't `itemInfo` at this point. Then, such an error would show up as a crash during development. We also find the error faster than in a case where we just return from `viewWillAppear(_:)`, and wonder why the UI is not populated with data.

To make the app crash in case there is no `itemInfo`, replace the `guard` statement with the following:

```
guard let itemInfo = itemInfo
  else { fatalError() }
```

How much code coverage is enough?

What value of code coverage is enough? This question cannot be answered because it mostly depends on the project and people working on the project. In fact, it is often better to ignore the code coverage data altogether, because it only has a limited value to decide whether tests are missing. But if you search the internet for this question, you will find a lot of different opinions on the topic. You might have to find your own answer to this question.

In my opinion, the one and only measurement to answer whether there are enough tests is your confidence. If you are confident that the code you've written is working because you've tested all the relevant aspects of it, then you have enough tests.

But, nevertheless, the code coverage data can help you figure out whether you have missed something in your test that you thought would have already been tested.

Automatic deployment with fastlane

Automatic deployment is the ability to create a beta or an App Store version of an app with just one click or command. It is of great benefit to be able to ship a version without all the hassle of provisioning profiles and code signing (often referred to as **code signing hell**). Felix Krause, a developer, started a project named `fastlane.tools` to make deployment on iOS as easy as running a command in `Terminal.app`. We will use fastlane in this section to set up the automatic deployment for our to-do app.

 To run the commands in this section, you need a paid developer account.

Installing fastlane

Go to `fastlane.tools` (put `fastlane.tools` in your browser) and follow the installation guide. We won't repeat the steps here because fastlane is still in active development, and the probability that the installation process changes before this book is published is very high.

Setting up

Open `Terminal.app` and navigate to the folder with the to-do project. Put in the following command, press *Enter*, and follow the instructions on the screen:

```
fastlane init
```

When you are asked if you want to set up `deliver` or `snapshot`, put in n for **No**. But we want to use sigh to automatically create and download provisioning profiles for the app. The next step is to add the app to your developer portal. Put the following command into `Terminal.app` and press *Enter*:

```
produce
```

You will be asked for the credentials of your Apple ID. The password you provide here will be stored in the keychain. When asked about the app name, put in a good name for the app. This name will be used to create the app in iTunes Connect. If there is already an app with that name in the App Store, fastlane will tell you so. In this case, run `produce` again and choose another name.

Before we can create a beta build and load it to TestFlight, the app needs an icon file that is 120 x 120 in size. Create your own icon.

Add the icon by navigating to **Assets.xcassets** | **AppIcon** | **iPhone App iOS 7-10 60 pt** | **2x**.

To create a beta build and load it to TestFlight, use this simple command:

```
fastlane beta
```

Fastlane fetches the required provisioning profile, builds the app, and loads it into TestFlight. The whole process takes a while. But, everything runs automatically and you can do something else until the upload is finished.

If this is your first upload, fastlane will print something like this:

```
This build could not be used for external testing because the build is not
approved.
```

You can now open iTunes Connect, and submit the build for a beta review. This is how you can perform automatic deployments using fastlane.

Among others, fastlane is also able to upload the App Store description and screenshots for your app, and it can submit these for review. Take a look at the GitHub page `https://github.com/fastlane/fastlane` to obtain some knowledge about the many different tools in fastlane and how they can help you with your day-to-day development tasks.

Summary

In this chapter, you learned how to activate code coverage. You used the data from a measurement to improve your code. By activating the presentation of the coverage data in the editor, you figured out which lines aren't tested by the test suite.

Finally, you used fastlane to automatically create and load provisioning profiles and build and submit our app for the TestFlight review.

In the next and final chapter, we will discuss what you can do to learn more about testing and the other approaches that are included in writing tests.

8

Where to Go from Here

You learned how to write tests for models, view controllers, and networking code using the TDD workflow. Of course, an introductory book can only cover an overview of the wide topic of TDD.

There is more to learn (as always). This chapter starts with a recap of what we have covered in the book so far. Then, it'll go on to describe certain possible topics that you can take a look at next.

This chapter covers the following topics:

- What you have learned so far
- Integration tests
- UI tests
- Behavior-Driven Development
- TDD in existing projects
- More information on TDD

What you have learned so far

In the course of this book, we have mainly written unit tests. As the name suggests, unit tests test small units in isolation. The advantage of using unit tests for TDD is the immediate feedback that is received in the TDD workflow. We wrote a test, ran it, and immediately got a feedback about the status of our code.

We used mocks, stubs, and fakes to separate the units from the rest of the code. This allowed us to focus the tests on one microfeature at a time.

Using TDD, we build a model, view controller, and the network layer of our app. Next, we put all the parts together to form a real iOS app. We have seen how to use UI tests to implement functional testing that focuses on individual features rather than units.

Finally, we also used fastlane to automate the deployment process.

But, as you might have guessed, there is more. This book is, at best, only the beginning of your journey towards becoming a testing expert. The next few sections will give you some guidance on where you can go in order to gain more experience in testing.

Integration tests

In Chapter 6, *Putting It All Together*, we saw that unit tests could only test microfeatures in isolation. The next step would be to use **integration tests** to make sure that individual features play well together. In integration tests, you do not mock other components. Instead, you use the real implementation and write tests that make sure that the different parts of the codebase interact with each other in the way you anticipated.

You can also use XCTest to implement integration tests. But the setup is more complicated than in the tests we have seen in this book. You use real classes and structs, and even network requests can fetch real data from a web service. What makes integration tests more complicated is that you don't want to change data in a real database during the test. This means that everything you do in the test has to be reverted when the test is finished. Or, you may have to use a different database or web service for the test.

The disadvantage of integration tests in respect to unit tests is that it is much harder to find the reason for a failing test. This means that integration tests are complementary to a unit test suite. Integration tests should only fail because of an error in the integration, not because one of the units has a bug. So, you should not skip writing unit tests.

UI tests

We have written one UI test in Chapter 6, *Putting It All Together*, to implement a functional test for the input of new to-do items. But, the other features of the UI aren't tested yet. Unit tests can test whether an element is on the screen, but doing this is cumbersome. It is much easier to use the new UI tests that were introduced in Xcode 7.

As you may have already noticed, UI tests are slow. They need to start the app and wait until the UI is loaded before they can interact with it. In addition to this, the app is closed and reopened after each test to make sure that each test starts with a defined state. As a result, you should not test each UI element in isolation. You'd rather write tests for a complete function of the app (for example, adding a to-do item to the list).

In the case of the *ToDo* app implemented in this book, a useful UI test would test whether a to-do item can be checked on the list and if a user can show the details of a to-do item. Go ahead, add the tests yourself using the recording feature of Xcode.

But, as described, you should add a separate scheme for the UI tests to keep the main testing suite fast.

Behavior-Driven Development

Behavior-Driven Development (**BDD**) is sort of similar to TDD, but you can focus on testing the behavior of your app instead. The main difference is the way the tests are written. Using XCTest, you mainly use the method name to describe what the test does. BDD frameworks usually allow you to write the expected behavior as a text string and therefore make the tests easier to read.

It is often said that the tests become so clear that people who are not familiar with programming can write them. Here is an example that uses the **Quick** framework and its matcher framework, **Nimble**:

```
class ToDoItemSpec: QuickSpec {
   override func spec() {
     describe("to-do item") {

       it("can be created with a title") {
         let item = ToDoItem(title: "Test title")
         expect(item).toNot(beNil())
       }

       it("can be created with a title and a description") {
         let item = ToDoItem(title: "Test title",
                          itemDescription: "Test description")
         expect(item).toNot(beNil())
       }
     }
   }
}
```

These two tests are equivalent to the one that we wrote in Chapter 3, *A Test-Driven Data Model*:

```
func testInit_ShouldTakeTitle() {
  let item = ToDoItem(title: "Test title")
  XCTAssertNotNil(item)
}
```

```
func testInit_ShouldTakeTitleAndDescription() {
  let item = ToDoItem(title: "Test title",
                   itemDescription: "Test description")
  XCTAssertNotNil(item)
}
```

Quick can do a lot more to make your tests easier to read. Search for Quick on GitHub and see yourself. Even if you don't want to use BDD, the Quick documentation has a lot of general and valuable information about testing.

TDD in existing projects

You most probably already have projects that have been implemented without any tests. It is much harder to add tests to an existing project than it is to write them first. When you don't keep in mind that you need to write a test for code sometime in the future, the code itself will become hard to test. It is often easier to tie the different parts of the app together, instead of keeping them separated with a clear and defined interface to each other. As a result, it becomes hard to separate microfeatures in order to test them with unit tests. In addition to this, testing methods with many side effects can be cumbersome to deal with.

When writing the tests initially, you will automatically think about the tests. The code naturally becomes easier to test and more modular.

Back to your existing projects. What could you do to add tests? The way to go is to start small. Don't rewrite all the methods using TDD. This won't work, and you will most probably remove all the tests when you realize how hard this is.

Instead, when you find a bug in the code, try to write a failing test for the bug, and make the test pass. This way, you can improve your code, and make sure that this bug never returns without being noticed. Unfortunately, this method will not work all the time, as your code might have a lot of coupling. But you should try it anyway. Take some time to think about what you would have to change to make this feature testable.

A second approach is to add features using TDD. You may have many ideas about how you could improve your app. Let's say, in the example of the ToDo app, you would like to add the ability to share the number of to-do items on Twitter to show all your friends and followers how busy you are. Even if the app doesn't have any tests, we could break this feature into several micro features and write tests for them before we implement the code.

The most important thing is to start writing tests. The tests don't have to be perfect. In the beginning, a nonperfect test is better than no test. Later, you may realize that some of the tests could be improved and even deleted. That is not a problem. Just keep adding tests. The more tests you write, the better your tests will become.

Generating mocks with Sourcery

In this book, you created all the needed mocks yourself. You may have noticed that this is a boring task. Most mock classes consisted of mainly boilerplate code. Fortunately, there is a solution: Sourcery (`https://github.com/krzysztofzablocki/Sourcery`). From its GitHub page:

> "*Sourcery scans your source code, applies your personal templates, and generates Swift code for you, allowing you to use meta-programming techniques to save time and decrease potential mistakes.*"

There are many templates for common tasks that are ready to use. For example, there is a template to generate mock classes from protocols. Let's have a look how we could use Sourcery to generate a mock for `ItemCell`.

To enable Sourcery to generate the code, we need to add a protocol with the methods that should be mocked. Imagine, we want to generate a mock for the method `configCell(withItem:checked:)`. All we have to do is add the following protocol to `ItemCell.swift`:

```
protocol ItemCellProtocol: AutoMockable {
   func configCell(withItem: ToDoItem, checked: Bool)
}
```

In the Terminal, we run Sourcery like this:

```
path/to/sourcery --sources path/to/ItemCell.swift --templates
Templates/AutoMockable.stencil --output ItemCellMock.swift
```

The generated mock class looks like this:

```
// Generated using Sourcery 0.8.0
—https://github.com/krzysztofzablocki/Sourcery
// DO NOT EDIT

// swiftlint:disable line_length
// swiftlint:disable variable_name

import Foundation
#if os(iOS) || os(tvOS) || os(watchOS)
import UIKit
#elseif os(OSX)
import AppKit
#endif

class ItemCellProtocolMock: ItemCellProtocol {

  //MARK: - configCell

  var configCell_withItem_checked_Called = false
  var configCell_withItem_checked_ReceivedArguments:
  (withItem: ToDoItem, checked: Bool)?

  func configCell(withItem: ToDoItem, checked: Bool) {
    configCell_withItem_checked_Called = true
    configCell_withItem_checked_ReceivedArguments =
      (withItem: withItem, checked: checked)
  }
}
```

For most of the mocks you'll need, this might be enough. But even if you need something more, these generated mocks are a good starting point. In case you are really curious, you could generate your own template to generate exactly the code you need.

For more information about code generation with Sourcery, go to its GitHub page.

More information about TDD

You probably want to learn more about TDD and iOS. For example, we haven't discussed how to use TDD in an app using Core Data.

There are many blogs and screencasts on the internet about TDD and iOS (for example, `http://qualitycoding.org`, `http://iosunittesting.com` and `http://masilotti.com`). With the experience you have gained by reading through this book, you now have a good foundation of how to follow these articles and find your own testing style.

Maybe, by learning more about testing in iOS, you might start a blog to share what you have learned. I'm looking forward to reading about your experiments and findings. Let me know where I can find it. You can find me on Twitter at `@dasdom`.

Summary

This chapter gave you a short overview of the possible steps involved in becoming a testing expert. I hope you enjoyed reading the book as much as I enjoyed writing it. I also hope that you are eager to learn more about testing, in general, as well as TDD.

Index

CPSIA information can be obtained
at www.ICGtesting.com
Printed in the USA
FSHW02n0244260418
47460FS

9 781788 475709